WHAT IS FAITH?

HOW TO KNOW THAT YOU BELIEVE

CHRISTIAN QUESTIONS
VOLUME 3

WHAT IS FAITH?

HOW TO KNOW THAT YOU BELIEVE

J. D. MYERS

WHAT IS FAITH?
How to Know that You Believe
© 2019 by J. D. Myers

Published by Redeeming Press
Dallas, OR 97338
RedeemingPress.com

978-1-939992-60-4 (Paperback)
978-1-939992-61-1 (Mobi)
978-1-939992-62-8 (ePub)

Learn more about J. D. Myers by visiting RedeemingGod.com
Discover similar authors by visiting TheGracelings.com

Cover Design by Taylor Myers
TaylorGraceGraphics.com

JOIN JEREMY MYERS AND LEARN MORE

Take Bible and theology courses by joining Jeremy at
RedeemingGod.com/join/

Receive updates about free books, discounted books,
and new books by joining Jeremy at
RedeemingGod.com/reader-group/

WANT TO LEARN MORE?

Take the online Gospel Dictionary course
which defines 52 key words of the gospel.

One of the words in this course is "faith" but it also
defines words like salvation, sin, forgiveness, and grace.

Learn more at RedeemingGod.com/Courses/

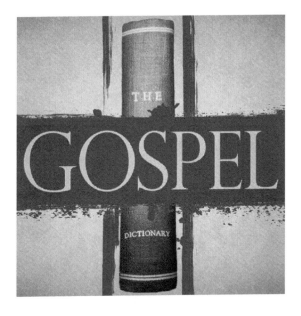

The course is normally $297, but you can
take it for free by joining the Discipleship Group at
RedeemingGod.com/join/

Other Books by Jeremy Myers

Nothing but the Blood of Jesus

The Atonement of God

The Re-Justification of God: A Study of Rom 9:10-24

Adventures in Fishing (for Men)

Christmas Redemption

Why You Have Not Committed the Unforgivable Sin

The Gospel According to Scripture (Forthcoming)

The Gospel Dictionary (Forthcoming)

Tough Texts on the Gospel (Forthcoming)

The Bible Mirror (Forthcoming)

The Grace Commentary on Jonah (Forthcoming)

Nin: A Novel (Forthcoming)

Studies on Genesis 1 (Forthcoming)

Studies on Genesis 2–4 (Forthcoming)

God's Blueprints for Church Growth (Forthcoming)

The Armor of God: Ephesians 6:10-20 (Forthcoming)

Books in the *Christian Questions* Series

Vol. 1: What is Prayer?

Vol. 2: What are the Spiritual Gifts?

Vol. 3: What is Faith?

Vol. 4: Am I Going to Hell? (Forthcoming)

Vol. 5: How Can I Study the Bible? (Forthcoming)

Vol. 6: Am I Truly Forgiven? (Forthcoming)

Books in the *Close Your Church for Good* Series

Preface: Skeleton Church

All books are available at your favorite bookstore.
Learn about each title at the end of this book.

For those who want to know that
they *really* do believe.

TABLE OF CONTENTS

INTRODUCTION TO THE "CHRISTIAN QUESTIONS" BOOK SERIES

This "Christian Questions" book series provides practical down-to-earth answers to everyday Christian questions. The series is based on questions that people have asked me over the years through my website, podcast, and online discipleship group at RedeemingGod.com. Since thousands of people visit the site every single day, I get scores of questions emailed in to me each month from readers around the world. Many of the questions tend to be around various "hot topic" issues like homosexuality, violence, and politics. Other questions, however, focus more on how to understand a particular Bible passage or theological issue. For example, I receive hundreds of questions a year about the unpardonable sin in Matthew 12.

I love receiving these questions, and I love doing my best to answer them. But after I answered the same question five or ten times, I realized that it might be better if I had a ready-made and easily-accessible resource I could invite people to read.

So the goal of this "Christian Questions" book series is to answer the questions that people send in to me. At this time, I do not know how many books will be in the series.

Below is the current list of books in the "Christians Questions" series. Most of these are not yet published, but I include the list to show you where the series is headed.

What is prayer?

What are the spiritual gifts?

Am I going to hell?

Why is the world so messed up?

Can God forgive my sin?

What is the unforgivable sin?

What is baptism?

What is the church?

What is repentance?

How can I evangelize?

What is faith?

Can I lose eternal life?

Why did Jesus have to die?

Should Christians keep the Sabbath?

What is demon possession?

How can I gain freedom from sin?

What is election and predestination?

Does God love me?

Why did God give the law?

Does God really want blood sacrifices?

What is sin?

What is the best bible translation?

Can I trust the Bible?

How can I study the Bible?

If you have a question about Scripture, theology, or Christian living that you would like answered, you may submit it through the contact form at RedeemingGod.com/about/ or join my online discipleship group at RedeemingGod.com/join/.

Some of these "Christian Question" books are available as free PDF downloads to people who join my online discipleship group.

Visit RedeemingGod.com/join/ to learn more and join today.

ACKNOWLEDGEMENTS

Thanks goes to my parents, Bill and Alana Myers, for buying me stacks of theology books when I was young. Books were all I ever wanted for Christmas and birthdays, and they accommodated my strange request with an overabundance of good reading. I am especially grateful for the books by C. S. Lewis and Josh McDowell, who show showed me that we have a reasonable faith.

Thanks goes as well to Bob Wilkin of the Grace Evangelical Society for being the first person in my life to explain that faith is certainty and does not come in degrees or percentages. I also want to thank Dave Anderson of the Free Grace Alliance for teaching about the Excel spreadsheet illustration for faith which I prominently use in this book.

I also must never forget the members of my Advance Reader Team who helped proofread and prepare this book for publication. Nizam Khan, Wesley Rostoll, Mike Edwards, David DeMille, Pete Nellmapius, Michael Rans, Taco Verhoef, Wickus Hendriks, John Flegg, Radu Dumitru, Bernard Shuford, Craig Duncan, Bernard Shuford, and Jim Maus, thank you for your help on my books. Please let me know how I can help you on any books or projects in the future.

Finally, and most of all, thanks goes to my wife, Wendy, who has never stopped believing.

FOREWORD

How many times have you heard an altar call and you walked down the aisle thinking, "This time I *really* believe"?

How many times have you been baptized, thinking, "I'm not sure I had genuine faith the last time, but now I feel like I mean it"?

How many times have you been confused about the nature of faith and wondered if you were just a hypocrite in disguise?

Isn't that tragic?

Would you like to be sure that you believe?

After all, the New Testament calls Christians "believers" (1 Tim 6:2). And no wonder. Your eternal destiny turns on your faith in Christ. Jesus promised everlasting life to whoever would simply believe in Him for it (John 3:15-18, 36). That's as simple as the offer of eternal life gets ... assuming you know what it means to believe in Jesus!

Sadly, not everyone does.

In fact, there is widespread confusion about the nature of faith. And that means there is also widespread confusion about the nature of the message of eternal life.

You see, the doctrine of eternal life by faith alone has always been under attack in obvious ways. Through the centuries, many denominations and teachers have openly added works, rituals, sacraments, ascetic practices, and spiritual encounters to the one condition of receiving everlasting life.

But a more subtle kind of attack has also been underway.

Rather than openly teach that eternal life is by faith plus works, this strategy has tried to redefine faith itself to include good works. Hence, I have often heard preachers publicly claim to believe in justification by faith apart from works, and deny a works-based gospel, but when they were asked what it means to believe, they answered: "If you *really* believe, then you'll *do* this ..."

Belief became behavior.

In that way, works get smuggled in through the back door.

Do you see that teaching eternal life "by faith *plus* circumcision" and teaching eternal life "by a faith *that* circumcises" is a distinction without a difference? The result is the same either way: works become part of the condition of receiving eternal life.

Both are false gospels.

Hence, to defend the gospel, you have to defend

faith itself.

In the recent past, Gordon H. Clark's book *Faith and Saving Faith* helped to clear away the fog that has surrounded the nature of believing. Clark explained that to believe is to understand and to be persuaded that a proposition is true. But Clark's book had some faults. He was mostly concerned with the statements of other theologians in the Reformed tradition, making it less accessible to the general public. And Clark himself was unsure of what you needed to believe to receive eternal life. Clark advanced the cause, but there was further to go.

I tried to present a modern defense of Clark's position in my book *Beyond Doubt: How to Be Sure of Your Salvation.* However, since that book was not directly about the nature of faith, I had planned to write another on the topic. It is with a mixture of relief, sadness, joy, and not a little envy that I can say Jeremy beat me to it!

And he's done an excellent job.

In *What Is Faith?,* all the most common doubts, questions, concerns, and objections about faith are treated concisely, clearly, and biblically, using simple language anyone can understand.

If the message of eternal life by faith apart from works is to prevail in the churches today, we need to be clear about the nature of faith itself. We need the message of this book to be more widely known.

Whether you're confused about your faith or currently take a different position on how faith should be defined, you should read this book. I think Jeremy can persuade you to change your mind.

–Shawn Lazar
Editor of "Grace in Focus" Magazine and Radio
Author of *Beyond Doubt* and *Chosen to Serve*

AUTHOR'S PREFACE

When I was a teenager, I read the books *Know What You Believe* and *Know Why You Believe* by Paul E. Little. I found them to be helpful as a basic introduction to Christian doctrine and apologetics. I believed what I read (most of it, anyway). But then I read some other books which began to challenge my beliefs. Specifically, the ideas in these other books made me begin to wonder if I had *really* believed. They talked about "head faith" vs. "heart faith" and how our faith must be a "living and active faith" rather than a "dead faith." After all, we should all make sure we don't have the faith that demons have (Jas 2:14-26). These books challenged me to move beyond a mere "intellectual faith" based on "mental assent" and instead develop a "real faith."

As a result of reading these later books, I began to worry. How could I know if I had really believed? The question was critical, for my eternal destiny hung in the balance. If I only had a "temporary faith," a "spurious faith," or a "head faith" then I could think my whole life that I was headed for heaven, and would only discover after death that I ended up in hell ... when it was too late. So how could I know? More importantly, how could I know *now*?

I eventually discovered answers to all such questions.

This book shows what I learned along the way.

If you have similar questions as the ones I had, this book will help you find the answers. If you seek to not only know what you believe and why you believe, but also *that* you believe, this book is for you. Don't believe me? Read it and see!

INTRODUCTION

How often have you heard someone say that "Salvation is by faith alone, but not by a faith that is alone"? Or how about this one: "You can't say that salvation is by faith alone! After all, even the demons believe!" And of course, we must not forget the famous evangelistic appeal about missing heaven by eighteen inches because you have "head faith" instead of "heart faith." As a result of statements like these, many people struggle with whether or not they have believed.[1]

With all this confusion about faith, it is no wonder that when people hear that Jesus gives eternal life to anyone and everyone who simply and only believes in Him for it, some object by saying, "Yes, but how do I know if I've *really* believed?" Some people are afraid of having dead faith, little faith, empty faith, head faith, false faith, or temporary faith. Others wonder if they have believed the right things, or believed enough. Oth-

---

[1] Robert N. Wilkin, *Confident in Christ: Living by Faith Really Works* (Irving, TX: Grace Evangelical Society, 1999), 12f.

ers think that their actions prove that they never really had faith in the first place.

And on and on it goes.

The problem with this general befuddlement about faith is that it leads to uncertainty about where people stand in their relationship with God. Since eternal life is given to those who believe in Jesus for it, a person cannot really know whether or not they have eternal life if they cannot first know that they have believed in Jesus for it. So where there is uncertainty about faith itself, there is also uncertainty in the object of faith (Jesus) and the promise of faith (eternal life). In other words, Jesus's promise to give eternal life to those who believe in Him for it (John 3:16; 5:24; 6:47; etc.) is worthless if we cannot know whether or not we have believed. It is pointless to say that eternal life is by faith alone in Christ alone if we don't know what faith is.

For these reasons, the word "faith" may be one of the most important words in the Bible. The word is not only used in numerous passages and a wide variety of contexts, "faith" is also said to be instrumental in how we receive eternal life. Beyond simply receiving eternal life, faith is also taught to be a key element of living the Christian life as a follower of Jesus. In other words, we not only receive eternal life by faith in Jesus, but we live out our Christian life by faith as well. Numerous other truths of Scripture are also experienced and applied by faith. This is why faith is so important. It allows us to gain eternal life, live the Christian life, and better understand Scripture.

If you have ever struggled with the question of whether or not you *really* believe, or whether or not you are *truly* a Christian, this book is for you. By reading this book, you will learn how faith is defined in Scripture. Once you learn this, you will discover that you can *know* that you have believed, and therefore, *know* that you have eternal life through Jesus Christ. You don't need to wonder any longer. You don't need to fear that maybe you didn't believe *enough*. Yes, you can know for sure that you have believed in Jesus for everlasting life. Best of all, you can know today.

Toward this end, the following book will clarify what the Bible teaches about faith. Chapter 1 will define faith according to how the word is used in Scripture and how it is defined in the lexicons. Chapter 2 will then discuss how we come to believe things. Understanding what faith is and how faith operates will then enable us to clarify some of the prevalent misconceptions about faith (Chapter 3). Once all this is cleared up, Chapter 4 reveals how to know that we actually do believe. The book then closes out in Chapter 5 by applying all of these insights about faith to various passages from Scripture.

So are you ready to discover what faith is and whether or not you believe? We begin by defining faith.

CHAPTER 1

DEFINING FAITH

Almost everybody has heard the story of the man who walked across Niagara Falls on a tightrope. After the tightrope had been fixed in place, he started gathering a crowd to watch his daring and dangerous feat. "Come one! Come all!" he shouted into his bullhorn. "Watch me walk above Niagara Falls, balancing on nothing more than this little rope!"

As people started gathering, he passed around a sample of the rope so people could see how small it was. "One little slip, and I will tumble to my death in the waters below!" he shouted. "You never know when I might fall. The rope is getting wet from the misting water. A wind is coming up the gorge. I don't want to die, but today could be the day!"

As the crowd swelled even more, he shouted to those who had gathered, "Who believes I can walk across the falls and back without falling to my death below?"

Most of the crowd shouted that they believed he could do it. Many of them cheered him on to try it. So he climbed up onto the rope, and balanced his way across Niagara Falls. When he reached the far side, he turned around and came back. He didn't slip. He didn't fall. In fact, he barely wobbled or wavered. So when he returned to the safety of the shore, he motioned with his hands for the cheering crowd to quiet down.

"That was too easy!" he yelled. "That wasn't a challenge for me at all! Let's make it more difficult! Who believes I can do again, but this time, while pushing a wheelbarrow? If my hands are on the wheelbarrow, I will not be able to use them to balance on the rope. Shall I give it a try? Do you believe I can do it?" He motioned to a nearby wheelbarrow, which he had brought for this very purpose.

The crowd cheered their approval, which caused the number of gathering people to swell even further. So with the help of two nearby men, he lifted a wheelbarrow up onto the rope, and then started pushing it across the Falls. He went more slowly this time, and even had a few wobbles, which caused the crowd to gasp and cry out with fear, but he made it to the other side and back without any great problem.

The crowd went wild.

"That was too easy!" he yelled. "Who believes I can do it again, but this time, with another person inside the wheelbarrow?" The crowd roared their approval. "I would not only be risking my own life, but also the life of the person in the wheelbarrow," the man shouted to the crowd. "With a show of hands, let me see how many of you believe I can do this!" Almost every person in the large crowd raised their hand. It was nearly unanimous.

"Wonderful! I am so glad to see that you have such faith in me! I think I will give it a shot!" the man yelled. "Now … among all of you who raised your hand, do I have a volunteer to get into the wheelbarrow?" Every hand in the large crowd went down. "What?" said the man. "You've seen me walk across Niagara Falls twice without any problems, once while pushing this wheelbarrow! And most of you believe I can do it with someone else in the wheelbarrow with me! But when I ask which of you wants to get into the wheelbarrow, none of you volunteer? Do you believe I can do it or not?"

But there were no takers, so the crowd did not see him push someone across Niagara Falls in a wheelbarrow that day.

This story is likely fictional, but it is often used by pastors and preachers as an example of faith. They say, "You see? It's not true faith unless you get into the wheelbarrow. Those people didn't *really* believe. They just *said* they believed. They raised their hand claiming they had faith the man could do it. But it is not enough to *say* you believe. It is not enough to *claim* you have faith. If you *really* believe, you have to get into the wheelbarrow. Otherwise, you have false faith. Spurious faith."

Then the pastor goes on to tell the audience how they can have true and effective faith. Usually the pastor says that they need to "prove" the reality of their faith by their good works. If they don't have the good works which proves the existence of their faith, then they are just like the people who claimed to have faith, but didn't prove it by getting into the wheelbarrow. Most people go away from such a sermon wondering if they've *really* believed, and therefore, whether they are *really* a Christian.

But you can know that you are really a Christian and that you have really believed. You can know that you have eternal life. You can know that you are already in the wheelbarrow, and that it is the safest place you can be. This knowledge of your safety and security in Jesus Christ begins by properly defining the word "faith."

THE DEFINITION OF "FAITH"

When we begin to define the word "faith," it is important to recognize that modern, English usage of the word "faith" does not match the ancient Hebrew or Greek usage. The way this word is used today bears little resemblance to the way the word was used in biblical times.

The word "faith" is sort of like the word "love," though somewhat in reverse. In modern English, we have one word for love, and we use it in reference to a wide variety of objects, including sports, spouses, occupations, and vacations. But in Greek, as nearly everyone knows, there are four words for love. Each word has a different shade of meaning, and is used in reference to different types of objects. Yet when people do not know about the different types of love in the Greek language, and they read about "love" in the Bible, they might confuse the way the word is used in the Bible with how we sometimes use it today. Therefore, when the Bible talks about God's love for us, some people might think that God just temporarily "likes" us, as when a person "loves" a song they hear on the radio.

Something similar happens with faith, though in reverse. Greek only has one root word for faith, whereas English has several. The Greek noun is *pistis* and the verb is *pisteuō* (with the root for both being *pist-*),[1] but English Bibles tend to translate the first as "faith" and the second as "believe." Sometimes the noun even gets translated as "faithfulness," which most would agree is quite different in meaning than "faith" itself. Furthermore, there are even cases where the Greek word will get translated as "trust." So here we have one Greek root word, with at least four different English words used to translate it. For consistency, it might be best to use only one English root word as a translation for the one Greek

---

[1] It is no wonder that Christians argue so much about the nature of faith ... the Greek root is *pist*. So why are some Christians so angry when they defend their faith? Because they're *pist*. But that's okay. Since faith, hope, and love are the three greatest Christian virtues (1 Cor 13:13), this means that it is good to be *pist*. Ok, I'll stop now.

root. I suggest "belief" and "believing." This in itself would clear up a lot of the confusion about "faith."

But this would not clear up all the problems. Even if we take the main two English translations, "faith" and "belief," our modern English usage of these words does not come close to matching the ancient Greek usage. Today, when we talk about "faith" or "belief" we generally use the words as a synonym for hope. We might say, "I believe the Cubs will win the World Series this year," but we don't really know for sure that they will. In fact, such a "belief" is closer to wishful thinking.

Or we might say, "I have faith that the government will keep me safe." But this is closer to hope. There is a good chance that the government will do its job to protect us, but it cannot protect us from everything all the time, especially not from natural disasters and rogue terrorist attacks. In sentences such as these, the words "believe" and "faith" are equivalent to "wish" and "hope."

In light of these sorts of problems about faith, people get confused—and rightfully so—when they read about faith and belief in the Bible. They are not sure whether they should understand faith to be more like hope, wishful thinking, trust, faithful actions, or maybe something else.

A lot of the confusion arises from something Plato taught more than 2000 years ago. N. T. Wright summarizes it well:

Plato declared that belief was a kind of second-rate knowing, more or less halfway between knowing and not knowing, so that the objects of belief possessed a kind of intermediate ontology, halfway between existence and nonexistence. This way of thinking has colored popular usage, so that when we say, "I believe it's raining," we are cushioning ourselves against the possibility that we might be wrong, whereas when we say, "I know it's raining," we are open to straightforward contradiction. But this usage has slid, over the last centuries, to the point where, with a kind of implicit positivism, we use *know* and *knowledge* for things we think we can in some sense prove, and *believe* and its cognates for things that we perceive as degenerating into more private opinion without much purchase on the wider world.[2]

Whether or not Plato was right (and I don't think he was), his way of thinking about faith and belief is the way people use the words today. "Faith" is more of a hope, or a possibility, that something might or might not be true. In the minds of many, their beliefs do not need facts to back them up, and sometimes, their beliefs can even contradict the facts.

But this is not the way faith is described in Scripture or in the writings of early Christians. In the Greek New Testament, the word "faith" is most commonly used in reference to something that a person knows to be true. This is where N. T. Wright is headed in the quote

[2] N. T. Wright, *Surprised by Scripture: Engaging Contemporary Issues* (New York: HarperOne, 2014), 42-43.

above. For New Testament era Christians, to believe something, or to have faith, meant that they were persuaded or convinced of the truth of it. They *knew* it to be true. Good synonyms for "faith," therefore, are not "hope or wish" but rather "persuasion, conviction, or knowing."

New Testament Greek Lexicons such as BDAG typically provides three basic definitions for *pistis*. When used with an article, as in "*the* faith," it typically refers to the body of Christian beliefs that separates Christianity from other religious faiths. It is used this way thirteen times in the New Testament (cf. Acts 6:7; Rom 4:11; Gal 1:23). Second, the word can be translated as "faithfulness" or "fidelity." BDAG lists six possible verses with this meaning, but not all English translations of these passages translate it in such a way. In fact, "major contemporary English versions translate *pistis* as 'faithfulness' or 'fidelity' in only three or four New Testament verses."[3] And even these could arguably be translated as "faith" (Matt 23:23; Rom 3:3; Gal 5:22; Titus 2:10). This point will be discussed further in Chapter 4.

The third possible definition for *pistis* is also the most common. Over 180 times in the New Testament, *pistis* refers to "believing." In context, this belief occurs when a person knows something to be true based on the reliability of the one who teaches it. The last part of this

[3] Wayne A. Brindle, "Faith in Christ Does Not Mean Faithfulness or Fidelity," *Grace in Focus* (Jan/Feb 2018), 24. This article does an excellent job summarizing the lexical data for *pistis*.

understanding is critically important, as we will shortly see. This understanding is by far the most common way of defining and translating *pistis* in the New Testament, and is also closely related to the lexical definition of the Greek verb, *pisteō*.

Therefore, the primary lexical definition for the verb is "to consider something to be true, to believe."[4] Faith (and the verb "believe") is a confidence, persuasion, or conviction that something is true.[5] We have faith when we are fully persuaded by the evidence presented to us. "To believe is to be persuaded that some declaration is true. … If you think something is true, you believe it."[6] Joseph Dillow says,

> Faith is located in the mind and is persuasion or belief. It is something which "happens" to us as a result of reflection upon sufficient evidence … Saving faith is reliance upon God for salvation. It does not include within its compass the determination of the will to obey, nor does it include a commitment to a life of works. To believe is to be persuaded and be reliant and includes nothing else.[7]

[4] Walter Bauer et al., *A Greek-English Lexicon of the New Testament and Other Early Christian Literature*, 3rd ed. (Chicago: University of Chicago Press, 2000), 816.

[5] Wilkin, *Confident in Christ*, 5, 7.

[6] Shawn Lazar, *Beyond Doubt: How to Be Sure of Your Salvation* (Denton, TX: GES, 2017), 106.

[7] Joseph C. Dillow, *The Reign of the Servant Kings: A Study of Eternal Security and the Final Significance of Man* (Miami Springs, FL: Schoettle Publishing, 1992), 276.

Dr. Robert Wilkin, founder of the Grace Evangelical Society and author of numerous books, writes this about the definition of faith:

> Faith is the persuasion or conviction that something is true. In Acts 17:4 Luke tells us concerning Jews at the synagogue in Thessalonica. "And some of them *were persuaded*." Then in the next verse he reports, "But the Jews who were *not persuaded* … attacked the house of Jason …" A few verses later Luke reports on the response of the Jews at the synagogue in Berea: "Therefore many of them *believed* …" (v 12). Clearly *the persuasion* of vv 4-5 is synonymous with *the unbelief* of v 12. Faith is persuasion of the truth of a fact or proposition, in this case, that Jesus is the Messiah who guarantees everlasting life to all who believe in Him.[8]

So what then is biblical faith (or belief)? We can do no better at defining faith than does the author of Hebrews, who writes: "Faith is the substance of things hoped for, the evidence of things not seen" (Heb 11:1). The author of Hebrews is saying that faith substantiates, or sees as reality, that which we have previously only hoped to be true. Faith is the evidence, conviction, or confidence in things we cannot see. Certainly, we also believe the things we have seen, but the faith described in the rest of Hebrews 11 is the faith that is confident in

---

[8] Bob Wilkin, "Should we Rethink the Idea of Degrees of Faith?" *JOTGES* (Autumn 2006), 3.

God's promises based on what is known about God's character and God's Word.

FAITH IN THE PROMISES OF GOD

Many people struggle with thinking about faith as a persuasion or conviction that something is true because they have often discovered that their faith in humans is misplaced. They believe that someone is going to do something, only to discover later that this other person did not follow through on what they promised. So it is sadly true that we cannot always believe in humans for the promises they make.

But God is not a human that He should lie (Num 23:19). We can always believe in God for the promises He makes. This is why faith toward God is a certain and sure faith. Such faith is not about us, but is all about Him. Since faith is the confidence or conviction that something is true based on the evidence presented,[9] and since God can fully be trusted, faith in the promises of God is a sure and certain faith. So believing in the statements of God is the same as knowing with certainty that what God says is true.

[9] Cf. a similar definition in Grant Hawley, *The Guts of Grace: Preparing Ordinary Saints for Extraordinary Ministry* (Allen, TX: BoldGrace, 2013), 125. He writes, "… to have faith is to be persuaded that something is true. It is to be fully convinced that what God says is true."

But is believing in what God says the same thing as believing what Scripture says? In other words, although we can know for sure that what God says is true, does this mean that we can know for sure that what the Bible says is true? The answer is yes … and no. While we can always have *absolute* certainty in the promises, instructions, and ideas of God, an honest bit of self-reflection reveals that sometimes we humans do not always properly understand what God has said. There is often a difference between what God has said and what we humans *think* God has said.[10] Ideally, what the Bible actually says and what we think the Bible says should be the same, but this is not always the case. One goal of sanctification and Christian maturity is to find and discover where our understanding of God and His Word is wrong, and then change our views to match what is actually true.

So are the truth claims of Scripture absolutely true? Yes, they are, because they are of divine origin.[11] But since we humans often misunderstand what other people are saying, this means that it is also quite possible that we will misunderstand some of what God is saying through Scripture. While God is infallible and His Word can be trusted, we humans are not infallible, so

[10] See J. D. Myers, *How Can I Study the Bible* (Dallas, OR: Redeeming Press, 2019).

[11] Obviously, this depends on the inspiration and inerrancy of Scripture. If someone does not believe in inspiration and inerrancy, then their views of the reliability of Scripture will be much different.

that our understanding of God's Word cannot always be trusted. Therefore, to some degree, even when we are talking about our beliefs in what God has said in Scripture, it is wise to always retain a bit of humility, recognizing that maybe, somewhere along the way in our thinking and study, we might slightly (or greatly) misunderstand something about God and what He teaches in Scripture. God and His Word are infallible; our understanding of God and His Word are not.

Nevertheless, this is not to say that we cannot be certain about what we believe. We can. This is also not to say that our beliefs always contain an element of doubt. They don't. By definition, faith is the opposite of doubt (cf. Jas 1:6). If you doubt something, you don't believe it. When you doubt something is true, it is because you have not been presented with enough evidence to persuade or convince you that the statement or proposition is true. When you doubt, you don't believe. Indeed, when you doubt, you *can't* believe.

Are you confused yet? On the one hand, I say that our beliefs do not include any elements of doubt, but on the other hand, I argue that we cannot always be absolutely certain about our beliefs. So which is it? It is illogical to say that faith is certainty when it comes to the promises of God, but faith is uncertainty when it comes to the claims of humans. If we are going to properly define and understand faith, the definition of faith must stay the same whether we are talking about faith in God or faith in humans.

The solution is to recognize that while faith is indeed certainty, it might be best to think of faith as *reasonable* certainty.

FAITH IS REASONABLE CERTAINTY

Even though faith can be defined or understood as "knowing with certainty that something is true," this doesn't exactly mean that faith is *absolute* certainty. For example, when it comes to believing the truth claims made by other people, we may not always be absolutely certain that what they say is true or that they can follow through on what they promise. Unlike God, people are not infallible. People make mistakes. People have errors in judgment and logic. Unlike God, people are not omniscient, omnipresent, or omnipotent. And so there is a degree of uncertainty that sometimes enters into faith when we are dealing with beliefs that are not the promises of God. While I believe, and am persuaded or convinced, of the truth claim made by Einstein that $E=MC^2$, I also recognize the remote possibility that Einstein made a mistake and was therefore wrong.

This hesitancy to claim absolutely certainty about any particular fact is what causes some people to state that we cannot be *absolutely* certain about anything. But such reasoning reveals a misunderstanding about how

faith works, and how the various truths we believe inter-
act with one another. This interaction of beliefs will be
discussed further in the next chapter. For now, I am
willing to admit that when it comes to a discussion
about the certainty of our beliefs, it might be better to
speak of *reasonable* certainty rather than *absolute* certainty. Or maybe we could say that faith is educated and
informed certainty.

With this basic understanding of faith, note what we
have just discovered about faith. While faith (by definition) does not include any element of doubt, it is nevertheless true that doubt is often a pre-condition to faith.
In other words, it is quite often true that you cannot
believe something unless you first doubt it. Very often,
the only way you will investigate a particular truth is if
you first question it. Questions and doubt, then, are not
the enemy of faith, but the catalyst that leads to true
faith. In life and theology, your beliefs are not likely to
change unless you first question and doubt what you
believe. But this does not mean that faith includes an
element of doubt. There is a vast difference between
saying that faith follows doubt and faith includes doubt.

This means, of course, that doubt can actually be
healthy and helpful. Sometimes, it is only through
doubt that we come to properly believe. By doubting
and questioning the various truth claims presented to
us, we examine the reasonableness of these claims to see
whether or not they are true. And when we are persuad-

ed or convinced of their truthfulness, it is then that we come to believe them.

You have likely seen this in your own experience. All people are able to look back to the past and remember something they once wholeheartedly believed, but no longer do. There is no person in the world who has believed the same thing their entire life and never had any of their beliefs change. And if you think about how some of your beliefs changed, you will notice that they changed in one of two ways. Either you questioned what you believed and came to see that what you believed was wrong, or you questioned what someone else believed, and in the attempt to prove them wrong, discovered that they were correct after all. Either way, the act of questioning and doubting changed your beliefs.

But the process of questioning and doubting can also solidify your beliefs. When we question and doubt the things we believe, and then seek to find answers to these questions, we often end up realizing that what we believe truly does have a solid factual and logical foundation. During this process of questioning and doubting, we do not actually believe what we are investigating (for we cannot doubt and believe something at the same time), but the end result will either be a further solidification of this belief through additional facts and arguments to support it, or a rejection of this belief in favor of something else.

As you approach faith in this way, you will develop a humble confidence that what you believe, you believe because you have investigated the truth and understand the facts to the best of your ability. This doesn't mean that you have read every book, talked to every expert, and turned over every stone in your quest for certainty. It does mean, however, that you have a reasonable explanation for what you believe. And if part of these reasons is that you trust another person to have done the necessary research and work for you so that you believe what they tell you, then this also is a reasonable faith.

This is even true when it comes to faith in the promises of God. As suggested previously, while we can know with absolute certainty that everything God says is true, we cannot know with absolute certainty that we have properly understood everything God has said. But rather than say that faith is doubt (for the two are opposites), it is best to say that faith is *reasonable* certainty. And we gain this reasonable certainty through an ongoing questioning and thorough investigation into the vast network of beliefs that connect with and surround each and every other belief we hold. Again, we will discuss this idea more in the following chapter.

But let us first take what we have learned about faith and apply it to one of the most pressing questions that Christians have about faith. Many people wonder whether or not they have eternal life. Many wonder if they have *truly* believed. Now that we have a basic understanding of what faith is and how faith works, we are in a position to address this all-important question. Based on what we know about faith, we are able to know with certainty that we have believed, and therefore, also know with certainty that we have eternal life. Let us take these two points one at a time.

HOW TO KNOW YOU BELIEVE

Some people struggle with knowing whether or not they believe certain theological truths. Specifically, many people wonder whether or not they have believed in Jesus for eternal life. But before a person can know whether or not they have believed in Jesus for eternal life, they first need to know how to recognize faith (or belief) when they have it. That is, they need to know they have believed before they can know they have believed in Jesus for eternal life.

Strangely, it is usually only in this area that people struggle with knowing whether or not they have believed. People never wonder about whether or not they have *truly* believed other truth statements. For example, do you believe that 2+2=4? Of course you do. You know that this is a mathematical fact. Do you believe that the sun is hot and rain is wet? I hope so. These are scientific truths. Do you believe that Donald Trump was elected as the 45th President of the United States? Whether or not you like him, it is a historical fact that he was elected, so of course you believe it.

And how do you *know* that you believe these statements? You know that you believe them simply because you know that they are true. When you were a toddler, you didn't believe that 2+2=4, but you were taught this truth and came to believe it. You know that the sun is hot and rain is wet through personal experience. When you first heard that Donald Trump had been elected President, you might not have immediately believed it, but as the evidence was presented to you, you were persuaded or convinced by the evidence, and so came to believe it. So with all three statements, you believe them because you know they are true.

When it comes to theological truths, faith works exactly the same way. You know you believe something when you can substitute the word "know" for "believe." Thus, the statement "I believe that God exists" becomes "I know that God exists." The opposite is also true. If you do not know or if you doubt that God exists, then you do not believe that God exists.

So "belief" is just another way of speaking about knowledge. If you know something, you believe it. When someone says, "I believe that such and such is true" they were saying, "I know for a fact that such and such is true." Since faith is defined as a confidence, persuasion, or conviction that something is true, you can know that you have believed something if you know it to be true. So how do you know whether or not you believe something? You know you have believed something if you know it is true.

This understanding of faith is quite helpful when it comes to the central truth claims of Scripture, and especially the most important truth claim of all, which is that Jesus gives eternal life to those who believe in Him for it. If you know that this is true, then you know that you have eternal life. Let us consider this idea a little more carefully.

HOW TO KNOW YOU HAVE ETERNAL LIFE

There are numerous truth claims in Scripture related to the gospel. The central truth claim of the gospel is that Jesus gives eternal life to anyone who believes in Him for it (cf. John 3:16; 5:24; 6:47).

Although this central gospel claim is simple to understand, it is not easy to believe. That is, it is not easy to know that Jesus gives eternal life to everyone and anyone who simply and only believes in Him for it. In fact, this truth is so difficult to believe, most people don't believe it! Most people, even many within Christianity, believe that good works are somehow required in order to receive eternal life and entrance into heaven when they die. The human mind does not naturally know (or believe) that God freely gives eternal life to humans simply out of His love for them and grace toward them. We tend to believe the opposite instead.

So how is it that people come to believe in Jesus for eternal life? How is it that you can believe in Jesus for eternal life? More importantly, how is it that you can *know* that you have eternal life in Jesus? These are critically important questions.

To show you how these questions are answered, and therefore, how you can know that you have eternal life, let me present an alternate scenario. Imagine that your neighbor came up to you one afternoon, and told you that if you believed in him, he would give you eternal life. Would you believe him? I think not. Furthermore, it is unlikely that he could provide any amount of persuasive arguments that would convince you to believe in him for eternal life. It is a ludicrous claim. If he made such a claim, you would be more likely to believe that he was insane than to believe in him for eternal life.

Yet when someone knows nothing about Scripture or any of the historical and theological facts surrounding the person and work of Jesus, this is exactly what they think of the initial offer of eternal life for those who believe in Jesus for it. It literally sounds insane. If a person knows nothing about Jesus, and they are told that Jesus will give them eternal life if they believe in Him for it, their initial response might be "Who is this Jesus to make such a claim?" If they believe that there is no life after death, then they might have questions about eternal life, what it is, and why it is being offered. Their ability to believe this truth claim from Jesus might also require investigation into the existence of God, the issue of sin, why Jesus died on the cross, how we can know He rose from the dead, and what all this means in relation to His promise of eternal life.

Do you see how the simple truth claim that "Jesus gives eternal life to anyone who believes in Him for it" leads to a wide-ranging discussion about numerous other truth claims that must also be believed before someone will be persuaded or convinced to believe in Jesus for eternal life? So although the truth claim that Jesus gives eternal life to those who believe in Him for it is simple, it is not easy to believe. Before a person can be persuaded or convinced that what Jesus said is true, they must first come to understand and believe a whole host of additional and supporting truth claims that lead up to this central gospel concept.

In my book, *The Gospel According to Scripture,* I separate these gospel truths into various categories, such as Preparation truths, Proof truths, Presentation truth, and Purification truths.[12] The Preparation truths and Proof truths help lay the foundation and provide evidence for the truthfulness of the Presentation truth, which is that Jesus gives eternal life to those who believe in Him for it. The Purification truths are for those who have already believed in Jesus, and provide ways that we can

---

[12] J. D. Myers, *The Gospel According to Scripture* (Dallas, OR: Redeeming Press, 2019).

purify our lives and live in light of the eternal life we have been given in Jesus Christ.

Some people need to believe more of these Presentation truths; others need to believe fewer. Some people will believe various Preparation truths of the gospel based on the authority and trustworthiness of the person who taught it to them (such as a child believing what a parent says). In other cases, a person might need to investigate, research, analyze, and consider all the various arguments and ideas surrounding a truth claim before they come to believe it. Neither approach is better or worse than the other. But eventually, when a person comes to believe in Jesus for eternal life, it is because they have recognized the truth that Jesus has given them eternal life, not because they have earned it or deserved it, but because God loves them, forgives them, and accepts them into His family.[13] When a person comes to believe in Jesus for eternal life, it is because they have come to *know* that they have eternal life in Jesus.

This means that if you know that you have eternal life in Jesus, and not because of anything you have done, then you have it. It is that simple.

---

[13] God accepts and invites us into His life; we do not accept or invite Him into ours.

BELIEVE IN JESUS FOR ETERNAL LIFE

Let me offer a few points of clarification. First, note that people do not receive eternal life simply by faith alone. Yes, people receive eternal life by faith alone in Jesus Christ alone, but this is not the same thing as saying that eternal life is by faith alone. Do you see the difference? When it comes to receiving eternal life, the object of our faith is of paramount importance. One does not receive eternal life simply because they have faith. No, we receive eternal life by believing *in Jesus* for it. To believe in Jesus means to believe certain propositions about Jesus, namely, that Jesus is the sole provider and protector of eternal life.[14]

If eternal life were by faith alone, then everybody would have eternal life, for everyone believes something. Atheists believe that there is no God. They are persuaded and convinced that God does not exist. So even atheists believe. If eternal life is gained simply by believing, then atheists have eternal life. Similarly, it is not enough to have beliefs about the color of your car, the existence of the Milky Way galaxy, or the historical reality of Abraham Lincoln. People believe all sorts of things, but belief itself does not grant eternal life to anyone.

[14] Shawn Lazar provides some good clarification that the phrase "believe in Jesus" means to believe certain propositions about Jesus. See his article "Is Faith Trust in a Person?" https://faithalone.org/blog/is-faith-trust-in-a-person/ Last Accessed March 17, 2018.

Taking this a step further, it is not even enough to believe that God exists. For other than atheists, almost everyone believes in the existence of God (or gods). Muslims believe that Allah exists. Pagans believe in Odin, Thor, Loki, and others. Hindus believe in millions of deities. Though many Buddhists don't exactly believe in a god, they do believe that humans are working toward an infinitely divine, enlightened state of being. It is not even enough to believe in the God of the Bible, for many cults and religious groups believe in the existence of the biblical God.

Note that it is also not enough to believe that you have eternal life. Lots of people believe they have eternal life, but they believe in something other than Jesus for it. Maybe they believe that they have eternal life because they are "a pretty good person." In this case, they believe in their own good works for eternal life. Or maybe a person believes in the god of some other religion for eternal life. Here again, such people are not believing *in Jesus*, and therefore, do not have eternal life.

We can clarify even further. Lots of people believe all sorts of things about Jesus, and even say that they "believe in Jesus," and might also believe that they have eternal life. But many of these people do not believe in Jesus *for* eternal life. They believe all sorts of historical and theological facts about Jesus, but do not believe in Him for eternal life. They might correctly believe that Jesus existed, that He was God incarnate, that He lived a sinless life, died on the cross, and rose again from the dead three days later.

Such beliefs are good, important, and correct, but Scripture does not teach anywhere that those who believe such things will receive eternal life. After all, there are many people who believe many good things about Jesus, yet still believe that in order to receive eternal life they have to live a life of good works and faithful obedience to God. While such people do believe in Jesus and believe many things about Jesus, and may even believe that they have eternal life, they do not *believe in Jesus for eternal life*, but instead believe in themselves and their own good works for eternal life.

The bottom line truth of Scripture and the central message of the gospel is this: God gives eternal life to those who believe in Jesus for it (cf. John 3:16; 5:24; 6:47). Each word in the central gospel truth claim is important. We must believe in a person for a promise. Scripture invites us to believe that a person, Jesus Christ, can fulfill a promise, which is everlasting life. So do you believe that Jesus has given you eternal life? Do you know that you can have eternal life simply because Jesus promises to give it to you, and not because of anything you have done or will do? If you know this, then you have eternal life! Jesus guarantees it.

CONCLUSION

This brings us back to the illustration of the tightrope walker pushing a wheelbarrow across Niagara Falls. The people truly believed that the man could walk across the tightrope above Niagara Falls. They had seen him do it. They also believed that he could do it with a wheelbarrow. They had seen him do this as well. In both cases, their faith was real and genuine. Based on what they had seen him do, they also stated their belief that he would be able to push someone across Niagara Falls in a wheelbarrow. However, none of them were willing to get into the wheelbarrow themselves. Does this mean that they didn't actually believe? No, it does not.

First, walking across Niagara Falls on a tightrope has inherent risks. This is why it is so thrilling to watch. And given all the various things that can go wrong in such a situation—many of which are completely out of the control of the man on the tightrope—there is no guarantee that he will make it across. Even if he performed this feat a thousand times in a row and became so good at it that he could run across while blindfolded, there is still no guarantee that he would be able to do the one-thousand-and-first time. Maybe a stronger than normal gust of wind would knock him off balance. Maybe it would start to rain and he would slip. Maybe a reckless bird would hit him in the head. There are just too many variables.

No matter how many times the man completes this feat, it is a statistical certainty that eventually he will slip and fall to his death. So while the crowd could state their genuine belief every time that the man will make it across the falls, they also believe that a time will come when the man will fall. None of the people on the shore wanted to be in the wheelbarrow when that happened.

So the people on the shore had two genuine, but conflicting, beliefs. They believed that the man could walk across Niagara Falls, and would be able to do it many times, even with a person in a wheelbarrow. However, they also believed in statistics and science, both of which say that eventually, the tightrope walker will fall.

Related to this, while the people on the shore might have had full faith in the tightrope walker's ability to maintain his balance, none of them had faith in their own ability. It is logical and reasonable to think that the man could take someone across the Falls in a wheelbarrow if the person stayed completely still and did not move. After all, if the person in the wheelbarrow starts flailing about, screaming in terror, or even sneezes, such movement could throw off the balance, causing both people to plunge to their death below. And as all people know, we cannot always keep fear at bay, nor can we easily hold back a sneeze. Therefore, here again, while a person might properly believe that a well-trained tight-rope walker can push a person in a wheelbarrow across

Niagara Falls, there are too many unknown and uncontrollable variables for any person to believe that they themselves could hold still enough to complete such a dangerous journey.

The bottom line truth is that that this fictional illustration about how nobody from a watching crowd would get into a wheelbarrow so that they might be pushed across Niagara Falls on a tightrope does not illustrate the lack of faith in the watching crowd. To the contrary, it shows their true and genuine faith in a variety of truth claims. They believed the man could do it. But they did not believe in their own ability to sit still enough inside the wheelbarrow. They also knew (i.e., believed) that there were millions of random variables in nature that could create problems as well.

So did they believe the man could push a person across Niagara Falls in a wheelbarrow? Yes, they firmly believed that the man could do it. But did each individual person believe the man *would* do this for themselves if they got into the wheelbarrow? No, they did not believe this, for the various reasons mentioned above. They probably had somewhere over fifty percent certainty that he would, maybe even approaching ninety percent certainty in some cases. But this was not enough *reasonable certainty* for them to gamble their lives on it.

But notice how different it is when it comes to the promises of God made to us through Jesus Christ. God is not a tightrope walker who will eventually make a mistake if we just give Him enough time. If He promises to take us across a spiritual tightrope, He will fulfill that promise every single time forever and ever without fail. There are no spiritual or natural variables which can wreak havoc with the promises of God. The same goes for Jesus. When Jesus makes a promise, it is a promise with a 100% guarantee. Like God, Jesus is fully reliable.

Furthermore, many of the promises of God are not at all dependent upon our own effort or involvement. If we were to equate eternal life to getting into a wheelbarrow for a trip across Niagara Falls, then we would also have to say that on this trip, we could jump around and do flips inside the wheelbarrow and Jesus will still not lose His balance or let us fall into the waters below. We could even try to jump out, but He will not let us fall. Eternal life is His gift to us, and this gift has an everlasting guarantee. We are safe and secure in His hands, and He will never let us go (John 10:27-29). This is His promise. When we refuse to believe His promises, it is simply because we are refusing to believe that Jesus knows what He is talking about and can be trusted to do what He says.

Jesus is fully trustworthy and reliable. So you can believe in Him for what He says. And when He offers eternal life to anyone who believes in Him for it, you can know that if you have believed in Jesus, then you have eternal life. When you believe in Jesus, you are already in the wheelbarrow and He is taking you across the falls, and there is nothing that you, or anyone (or anything) else can do to stop Him (Rom 8:38-39).

Nevertheless, I imagine that you still have some questions about the nature of faith and how faith works. You also might still have some lingering doubts about whether or not you *really* believe. Maybe you have also heard people talk about head faith, heart faith, true faith, false faith, small faith, and great faith, and you want to know how these sorts of descriptions fit with what we have learned in this chapter. So the next chapter will continue to address the issue of how faith works, and specifically, how we come to believe something and why our beliefs can change.

CHAPTER 2

HOW FAITH WORKS

When my wife and I were newly married, we both served tables in a Mexican restaurant. One of the other servers was named Jesus Lopez (His first name followed the Spanish pronunciation "*Haysoos*"). But this Jesus we worked with was not very much like Jesus of the Bible. Jesus (the server) loved to work on Sundays when all the Christians came in to eat after their church services. He would go up to tables after they had finished praying over their meal and say, "I'm Jesus. Is everything okay?" (He would pronounce his name with the English pronunciation, "*Geesus*"). Most church-going Christians weren't quite sure how to respond.

But it was worse on Halloween. Those of us who served that night were supposed to dress up as some character. I don't remember what my wife and I dressed up as, but Jesus came dressed up as Satan. That night, while dressed as Satan and using the English pronunciation for Jesus, he greeted every table by saying, "I'm Jesus. I'll be your server tonight." Some tables laughed, while others looked shocked. I remember thinking that his statement bordered on blasphemy. Clearly, Jesus Lopez was nothing like Jesus Christ.

A few years later I was working as the pastor of a small church in Northwest Montana. One summer the church participated in a community children's outreach. I remember being shocked at the response of two neighborhood children (ages 8 and 10) when I asked them if they had believed in Jesus for eternal life. "Who's Jesus?" the older boy asked. Through further conversation, I discovered that they had never heard any story from the Bible about Jesus. They had also never heard about some of the other most famous Bible characters, such as Noah, Moses, or Jonah.

As I came to the realization that there were genuinely "unreached" people groups right in my own United States neighborhood, I thought about our fellow server from the Mexican restaurant. Imagine the response of these children if the only Jesus they knew had been Jesus Lopez. What would they have said, if they had never heard of Jesus Christ, but Jesus Lopez had been a teacher, friend, or neighbor? What would they have said if I invited them to "Believe in Jesus for eternal life"? Aside from his twisted sense of religious humor, Jesus Lopez was a nice enough guy, but I still think the children would have found it incredulous for some stranger to suggest that they "Believe in Jesus for eternal life." If Jesus Lopez was the only Jesus they knew, they would have looked at me like I was crazy. They were not ready (or able) to believe in Jesus because they didn't know or believe anything accurate about Jesus.

I share these two stories, and how they came together in my mind, as a way of illustrating how faith works. While it is absolutely true that Jesus gives eternal life to anyone who believes in Him for it, nobody in their right mind is going to believe in Jesus for eternal life unless they first know and believe many additional truths about Jesus.

What are these truths? Well, the set of necessary truths will be different for each and every person.[1] Consider the following statement: "Jesus is God." Do you believe this? (I do.) If you do believe this, have you ever stopped to consider *why* you believe that Jesus is God, or *how* you first came to believe it? (I have.) The belief that "Jesus is God" is an incredibly important belief for Christian life and doctrine. Our eternal destinies quite literally depend upon this truth.

So why and how do you believe that Jesus is God? You cannot say that you "Just believe it," for this is not true. Nobody is born into this world "just believing" anything. Quite likely, you initially came to believe that Jesus is God because some authority figure taught this truth to you. Maybe it was your parents or a Sunday

---

[1] I am *not* saying that each person has their own truth. I am not teaching relativism. I am saying that of all the *available* myriad of truths which support the claim that Jesus gives eternal life to those who believe in Him for it, different people will find different sets of truths persuasive. There is no single set of truths that will be persuasive for all people.

school teacher. It might have been a Christian pastor or author. Yet before you believed that Jesus is God, you first came to believe that there is a God, and also came to believe in the authority of Scripture. You likely also learned some of the basic Bible stories, including several stories about Jesus. There was a whole series of truths you came to believe before you believed that Jesus is God.

Furthermore, after you believed that Jesus is God, this belief was likely challenged in various ways and at various times throughout your life. During those times, you probably read some books or heard some sermons that provided a defense of this central Christian belief. Maybe you had an experience which helped solidify your belief that Jesus is God. Maybe this belief wavered, and you stopped believing it for a while, but eventually, came back to the realization that Jesus truly is God.

It is also possible that you have gone through several cycles of this sort of questioning, study, and solidification of your belief that Jesus is God. As you went through these cycles of solidification, it is not that you *didn't believe* before. You did. But these cycles of questioning and investigating help you shore up your belief that Jesus is God by addressing the questions and issues that could potentially undermine it. If you are unable to address or find answers for the issues and questions about this central belief, then you would likely stop believing it. Sadly, some people do indeed stop believing that Jesus is God.

Are you beginning to see how faith works? Are you starting to understand how we come to believe certain truths? Each individual truth we believe is built upon the foundation of other truths and is intricately connected to a wide network of related truths. One cannot believe something unless they first believe several of the foundational and preliminary truths, and if a person eventually stops believing some of these other foundational beliefs, then this change has a ripple effect through a large number of other related beliefs.

In my experience, before a person can believe in Jesus for eternal life, they will not only need to believe several truths about the identity and character of Jesus, they will likely also need to believe in the authority of the person who is telling them about Jesus, and also the authority of Scripture which contains these truths. Furthermore, they will likely need to believe that there is a God, that humans are sinners, and that we humans will in some way answer to God for how we live this life. There might need to be some sort of belief about life after death and also a basic understanding of why and how Jesus took care of our sin.[2] There is a whole set of

---

[2] As mentioned previously, my book *The Gospel According to Scripture* (Dallas, OR: Redeeming Press, 2018), refers to these truths as Preparation truths. These foundational gospel beliefs help *prepare* a person to believe in Jesus for eternal life.

truths that must be understood and believed before a person can believe in Jesus for eternal life.

Do you see how each individual belief is dependent upon and connected with a wide variety of other beliefs? There is not one colossal, all-inclusive, comprehensive "belief" that makes a person a Christian. While a person does receive eternal life at the moment they believe in Jesus for it, there are always a whole series of beliefs that lead up to (and follow) that moment when a person believes in Jesus. These various beliefs are all connected and intertwined to create a vast network of beliefs that shift and change as new ideas are understood and then either accepted or rejected.

This understanding of faith is getting somewhat complex, so let me provide an illustration which might better explain how this network of beliefs actually works.

THE GIANT EXCEL SPREADSHEET

In the previous chapter I defined faith as a certainty or conviction that something is true. Some do not like the idea of faith as certainty. For example, author and pastor Greg Boyd once criticized the idea that faith is certainty by comparing faith to a house of cards.[3] He argued that

[3] Greg Boyd, "Toppling the House of Cards," A Sermon by Greg Boyd, delivered on January 30, 2011 at Woodland Hills Church. See https://whchurch.org/sermon/toppling-the-house-of-cards/. Last Accessed February 24, 2018.

if we believe that our faith must be certain, then any time a challenge or question comes along which threatens this certainty, our entire belief system comes tumbling down like a house of cards. Boyd talks about his own experience with this, saying that every time he stopped believing something he had been taught as a youth, he felt like his entire belief structure collapsed like a house of cards, and he had to painstakingly rebuild it from the ground up.[4] Boyd rightly points out that this is a dangerous and damaging way to live life, and it leads many people to abandon or reject Christianity altogether.

While I share Boyd's concern for the spiritual health and vitality of others, he goes on in the sermon to teach that rather than define faith as certainty, it is better to allow faith to include an element of doubt. According to him, the inclusion of doubt into faith allows people to embrace their doubts without feeling that they need to reject all of Christianity. In this way, a person can still be a Christian even if they have doubts that Methuselah lived to be 969 years old. (This is the reason my grandmother gave for rejecting the Bible and Christianity.)

I completely agree with Greg Boyd that Christianity is not an "all or nothing" belief system. I completely agree that people should be able to have doubts. I always encourage people to question everything. However, none of this means that faith includes doubt, as Boyd

---

[4] Gregory A. Boyd, *Benefit of the Doubt: Breaking the Idol of Certainty* (Grand Rapids: Baker, 2013).

suggests. Faith is actually the opposite of doubt. You either doubt or you believe, but it is nonsense to say that you have a belief that you doubt. You either doubt something or you believe it; but you cannot do both simultaneously. Logically and linguistically, faith must be defined as certainty and conviction. And if you have certainty about something, you do not doubt it. When you do doubt, you do not have certainty, and therefore, do not believe.

So how then do we avoid the "house of cards" disaster that Greg Boyd talks about? Like Greg Boyd, I also know people who think that if they cannot believe that the world was created in seven 24-hour days, this means they must reject all of Christianity. I even know some Christians who teach this very thing! So I agree with Greg Boyd that we cannot have a "house of cards" faith in which all of our beliefs stand or fall together. But how can we avoid this if faith truly is defined as certainty?

The solution is to use a better analogy.

Rather than thinking about faith as a house of cards, a better analogy is to think about our network of beliefs as a giant Excel spreadsheet.[5] If you are not familiar with a Microsoft Excel spreadsheet, it is an accounting tool which contains a series of rows and columns. At the in-

[5] I first heard this analogy from Dave Anderson, a pastor in The Woodlands, TX, in one of his podcast sermons. I cannot recall which sermon it was in. I think he termed this idea "Spreadsheet theology."

tersection of each row and column, there is a "cell." This cell can contain a bit of data. For example, a cell could contain a number or some sort of mathematical calculation. Spreadsheets are usually set up so that as you enter data into the cells, it automatically makes calculations in other cells. Advanced Excel spreadsheets might contain thousands of cells set in a way so that a change in one single cell might affect the numbers or calculations in thousands of other cells. Each little change can have a ripple or cascading effect throughout the rest of the spreadsheet.

It is helpful to think about our network of beliefs in a similar way. We can think of our belief system as a giant Excel spreadsheet. But rather than numbers and math calculations, each cell contains an individual fact. Since there are a nearly infinite number of facts, this giant spreadsheet has a nearly infinite number of cells. "The sky is blue" is in one cell, "I exist" is in another, and "There is a God" is in third. Furthermore, just like on any complex Excel spreadsheet, nearly all the cells are interconnected by functions, so that when one cell changes, it causes a cascading, rippling effect throughout the rest of the spreadsheet.

If we think about our beliefs in this way, we can see that when it comes to each individual statement, we can either believe it or disbelieve it. We can either know it to be true, or we can doubt that it is true. We can either assent and agree with the statement in the cell, or dissent and disagree. While we will be reasonably certain about several statements on this spreadsheet, we will be either ignorant or uncertain about the vast majority of statements. And as we change what we think about any particular fact, this change will have a cascading, ripple effect through the related and connected cells on the spreadsheet of beliefs.

What this means is that as we come to believe new ideas, some of the beliefs which have not changed for decades might need to be reconsidered in light of new evidence. Therefore, while we can have reasonable conviction or confidence about the accuracy of any single cell (or belief), we nevertheless know that the content of that cell is based upon the ideas of other related cells, about which we are less confident. To put it another way, the complete confidence of one belief in one "cell" can be based upon less confident beliefs of other "cells."

This way of thinking about faith provides adequate responses to many of the objections that some pastors and theologians have to the concept of faith as certainty. Many who criticize the idea of "faith as certainty" seem to think that the entire system stands or falls together.[6] But this is not the true nature of faith. It is impossible for the entire system of faith to collapse. Instead, our beliefs constantly shift and change as additional information is presented to us, so that new beliefs are turned

---

[6] For example, see Peter Enns, *The Sin of Certainty* (New York: Harper Collins, 2016).

"On" in the spreadsheet while other beliefs are corrected and turned "Off."

If you are not fond of this "accounting" spreadsheet metaphor, you could also think of our network of beliefs as a giant network of walking trails that spans the entire globe. At each fork in the road there is a sign with a "fact" written on it. You can either believe or disbelieve this fact, based on everything else you know to be true. What you believe about that fact determines the path you will take next on the trail. Sometimes, your later beliefs cause you to circle back around to earlier beliefs so that they can be reconsidered. This doesn't mean you didn't believe this idea before. You did. But now that you are presented with new evidence, new ideas, and new beliefs, the turn in the trail leads you back to revisit some earlier beliefs so that you make different turns and head down different, unexplored paths. When you think about your beliefs in this way, you see that they do not make a house of cards that tumbles down around you when one belief changes, but rather a world of possibilities with each and every fork in the trail that opens up new vistas and horizons to explore.

Regardless of which analogy you prefer, the end result is the same. While many people fear the experience of changing their beliefs, it can actually be embraced as a journey into the great unknown. The investigation of truth is a quest to be enjoyed and anticipated. You can look forward to the changes and adjustments in your faith with great excitement. Each change is a little min-iature adventure. Yes, the first few times are scary. Yes, it sometimes seems like the floor dropped out beneath you, or that you jumped out of an airplane without a parachute. But if you trust the process you will soon discover that examining your faith is nothing more than the greatest roller coaster ride of a lifetime. Yes, your stomach may jump into your throat from time to time, but after a while, you begin to really enjoy the ride. Eventually, as you allow the doubts and fears to resolve, you soon discover that Christianity is a reasonable faith, that there are answers to all questions that might come, and that no matter what, God will never let you fall.

Best of all, with each cell that changes (or fork in the trail that you travel) you gain a spreadsheet (or trail map) that is more accurate than it was before. One of these truths you discover quite soon (if you allow God to teach it to you), is that God does not require a spreadsheet of beliefs that is free of error. Quite to the contrary, He desires a spreadsheet of beliefs that is con-stantly shifting and changing as we bring our life and thoughts into conformity with Jesus Christ and the revelation of Scripture. But this is a process, a journey, or an adventure that will last a lifetime (I suspect this adventure will last into eternity as well, as we forever unravel the infinite mysteries of glorious vistas of God), and so God is patient with us as we fill out our spread-sheet of beliefs with Him by our side.

Viewing faith in this way helps you see that although one changed belief often does cause a change in many other related beliefs, your entire belief system never collapses like a house of cards. It may initially feel like this has happened, but by taking a deep breath and examining the new evidence you have been given, you will discover that most of your beliefs remain intact. You will also discover that you now have a better and more accurate belief system through which to view God, Scripture, yourself, others, and life in general.

THE SPREADSHEET AT WORK

Let us briefly see how this works with the truth claim that "Jesus gives eternal life to those who believe in Him for it." I believe this truth with absolute certainty. I have many reasons for this belief, all of which reside in their own individual cells. For example, I believe that there is a God, and that only He gets to decide who has eternal life with Him and how they get it. I furthermore believe that Jesus is God, and so He knew what He was talking about when He offered eternal life. I also believe that the Bible can be trusted as an authoritative revelation from God. I believe that I have properly understood the simple promises of Jesus to give eternal life to those who believe in Him (cf. John 3:16; 5:24; 6:47). I believe that Jesus does not lie. I believe that I am not able to earn or work for my eternal life on my own, because I can never be good enough to qualify for God's perfect standard of complete righteousness. If all these things are true, as I believe they are, then it is completely logical to be convinced and persuaded that Jesus gives eternal life to those who believe in Him for it. And since I believe in Jesus, I know that I have eternal life.

But if any of these beliefs were to change, then this would likely cause me to stop believing that Jesus gives eternal life to those who believe in Him for it. If I stopped believing that God existed, or that the Bible accurately records the teachings of Jesus, I might stop believing in Jesus for eternal life. However, the more I study and learn, the more evidence I find that supports all these beliefs. I now know too much to turn back on any of these truths and cannot imagine a situation that would cause me to reject them. The more I study and learn, the more beliefs I gain, each of which further supports the belief that Jesus gives me eternal life.

Is it possible that the authors of the Gospels failed to accurately record what Jesus said? It's possible, but not likely, so I don't believe this. Is it possible that those who copied the Bible and passed it down through the generations made a mistake? It's possible, but manuscript evidence proves that this is unlikely, and so I don't believe it. Is it possible that I have incorrectly understood what Jesus said and meant? Well, this is the most likely factor that could cause me to stop believing in Jesus. But since the teachings from Jesus about how to receive eternal life are some of the simplest teachings He gave (even a child can understand and believe these promises), I do not think this is likely, and therefore, I believe I have properly understood His promises.

Since my belief in Jesus for eternal life is based on a large number of other reasonable beliefs, if any one of these other beliefs were to change, there would indeed be a cascading effect of changing beliefs. As numerous beliefs changed, it might indeed feel like Greg Boyd's house of cards, as if everything I thought I knew was tumbling down around me.

However, note that there are many beliefs that can safely change without affecting my belief in Jesus whatsoever. My belief in Jesus is not affected at all by belief (or lack thereof) that Methuselah lived to be 969, that the universe was created in seven 24-hour days, or that Jesus is going to return in the future to slaughter all His enemies with a reign of terror and blood (I actually don't believe this). These beliefs can change back and forth numerous times (as they have over the years), but such changes will not cause my entire belief system to come tumbling down like a house of cards. Note that if someone feels that changes in these beliefs *will* cause their entire belief system to come tumbling down, this is likely because they believe the false idea that "All Christian beliefs stand or fall together." As soon as a Christian stops believing this, they will be able to investigate their beliefs with freedom and joy.

Now the same sort of belief changes can be observed even with beliefs that are not "theological." The "network of belief" concept applies to any individual belief. For example, I believe the sky is blue because I believe I know what "blue" is, and because I believe my eyes are not deceiving me. I furthermore believe that I truly exist in this world rather than in a dream world or computer simulation as in "The Matrix." Since all of these are reasonable beliefs, I can confidently believe (know) that the sky is blue.

However, if someone could persuade me that I did not exist, or that this world was a computer simulation, or that I have color-blindness and so do not accurately understand "blue," then I might realize that I am wrong about the blueness of the sky. But until these other beliefs change (which is extremely unlikely), I am fully confident that the sky is blue. (Keep reading, because later in this chapter, I do, in fact, stop believing that the sky is blue. I will even show you how it happened, which might convince you too.)

So based on this understanding of our beliefs as a vast network of truths about which we have reasonable certainty, we are able to discover five foundational truths about any one particular belief. In other words, since each belief depends and relies upon various other beliefs, but also affects and influences numerous other beliefs, this reveals five facts about how faith actually works. Some of these five truths about faith were briefly mentioned above, but let us consider each in more detail.

1. THERE ARE NO DEGREES OF FAITH

When we begin to think of our network of beliefs as a vast Excel spreadsheet, we realize that there is no such thing as "degrees" of faith. In other words, you cannot "partly believe" something. If you only "partly believe" something, then you do not yet believe it. Since each individual cell contains a single factual statement, you can only agree or disagree with that statement. You either know that it is true, or you don't. If you know it is true, then you believe it. If you don't know, or are unsure that the statement is true, then you don't believe it.

At the risk of mixing metaphors, you could think of each individual belief as a light switch. The switch (or belief) is either "On" or "Off." And there are no dimmer switches to faith. You either believe something or you don't. Individual beliefs do not come in "quantities." You cannot have 50% faith, or even 99% faith about a particular statement. Yes, various passages from Scripture talk about having "great faith" or "small faith" (cf. Matt 8:10, 26), but such texts should not be understood as referring to degrees or percentages of faith.[7]

---

[7] For an excellent explanation of the difference between great faith and little faith and many of the passages that are often used to defend the ideas of "degrees of faith," see Bob Wilkin, "Should We Rethink the Idea of Degrees of Faith?" *JOTGES* (Fall, 2006),

Instead, "great" faith occurs when people believe something that is hard to believe, while "small" faith occurs when they don't even believe things that are easy to believe.[8] This concept will be discussed later in more detail.

To apply this to the spreadsheet analogy, since each individual belief resides in its own cell, you can either believe or disbelieve the statement of that cell. In computer terminology, the cell is either a "0" or a "1." There are no decimals or percentages in the Excel spreadsheet of beliefs. If you lack confidence about the truth of a certain cell, then you don't believe it, and it is "Off." Quite often, the reason you do not believe the statement within that cell is not because of the content of the cell itself, but because it relies upon and is related to the beliefs and statements of other supporting cells. Similarly, this "Off" switch blocks you from believing other ideas down the line, which depend on your belief in the original cell. This idea about the interplay of the various cells on the spreadsheet helps us see the second truth about our beliefs.

https://faithalone.org/journal/2006ii/01%20Wilkin%20-%20great%20faith.pdf Last Accessed April 2, 2008.

    [8] For more on this, see the article I published on this topic here: Jeremy Myers, "Now That's Faith!" Grace in Focus Newsletter (January-February 2008). http://www.faithalone.org/magazine/y2008/faith.html Last Accessed July 20, 2014.

2. THERE ARE COUNTLESS TRUTHS WE CAN BELIEVE

The second truth about the network of beliefs, or our spreadsheet of faith, is that there are countless cells on this spreadsheet. Since there are a nearly infinite number of possible beliefs, there are countless statements we can either believe or disbelieve. And since each cell is either "On" or "Off," what we believe about the statement in that cell leads us to go one way or the other for all connected beliefs.

Consider again my earlier example of the statement "The sky is blue." This statement depends on me believing that I exist and that I can actually see. It depends upon me knowing that the sky actually exists. It depends on me knowing what the color "blue" is. It depends on me believing I have a decent grasp of the English language so that I know what the four words "They sky is blue" all mean.

Furthermore, if, for some reason, I come to believe that the sky is not blue, then this could have ramifications on other connected beliefs. For me to stop believing that the sky is blue, maybe I would have to believe that the sky was a giant TV screen set up by aliens. Or maybe (as some of the ancients believed) that we were actually living inside a giant bubble, and the sky wasn't sky at all, but was water, which helped them explain why rain fell from the sky. Do you see how changing one belief causes you to change others?

In fact, immediately after writing that previous paragraph, I decided to do some quick research to see if the sky really was blue. It turns out it isn't! The sky is not blue after all! It's violet.[9] But our eyes are unable to see the particular type of violet that is the color of the sky, and so it appears "blue" to us. Therefore, I now believe that the sky is violet. The science behind this fact persuaded me of this truth.

But as this belief changed in my mind, I did not observe all my other beliefs tumbling around me like a house of cards. Instead, my network of beliefs quickly adapted and adjusted to the new information I received, and (as far as I can tell), I only had to change a few minor other beliefs to accommodate this new belief. As a result, I now believe some ideas I did not believe before. I now believe that our atmosphere scatters the violet wavelength of light more than the other colors, and so the sky is violet. But since human eyes only have red, blue, and green receptors, we have trouble seeing the violet wavelength of light. So although the sky is violet, we see the violet sky as blue.

As a result of this little experiment, I have now switched the cell "Off" which says "The sky is blue" and switched "On" the cell which says "The sky is violet." However, the cell which says "I see the sky is blue" is

---

[9] Brian Koberlein, "Earth's Skies are Violet, We Just See Them as Blue," https://www.forbes.com/sites/briankoberlein/2017/01/11/earths-skies-are-violet-we-just-see-them-as-blue/ Last Accessed March 9, 2018.

still turned "On" for that belief has not changed. Though the sky is scientifically violet, our eyes observe it as blue.

Don't be confused by all of this. The point is to show you that there is a nearly infinite number of beliefs on your spreadsheet of faith, with each possible statement residing in its own cell. As you consider each individual statement, such as "The sky is blue," your assent (or lack of assent) to that statement both depends upon and influences numerous other beliefs on the spreadsheet. As your beliefs change and evolve, your spreadsheet is modified to accommodate these changes. This introduces a third truth about our beliefs.

3. SOME THINGS ARE EASY TO BELIEVE; OTHERS ARE HARD

Earlier in this chapter, it was stated that there are no such thing as degrees of faith. We either believe something or we don't. A cell is either "On" or it is "Off." If you are uncertain or unsure about a particular statement, then you don't believe it.

Some people think that the Bible does teach about degrees of faith because it occasionally mentions "little faith" and "great faith" (cf. Matt 6:30; 8:26; 14:31; 16:8; Luke 4:14-30; 12:28). There are also numerous passages in the Bible which seem to indicate that we must have "enough faith" before God answers our prayers (cf. Matt 13:58; 21:22; Mark 11:24; Luke 7:9, 50; 18:42; Jas 5:15-16). If there are no degrees of faith, then what do these descriptions of faith mean?

These descriptions refer to the fact that some truths are easy to believe while others are difficult. Since faith is the conviction or persuasion that something is true, people who have little faith have not been persuaded or convinced of even the basic truths, whereas, people who have great faith have been persuaded or convinced of some of the hard and difficult truths which few people come to believe. You and I do not have faith containers in our souls which overflow when our faith is great, but are nearly empty when our faith is little. Faith does not work like that. Great faith and little faith have nothing to do with the *size, amount,* or *degree* of faith. Rather, the terms "great faith" and "little faith" describe the difficulty of the truths that are believed. "Great faith is not some higher level of conviction. It is believing something that is harder to believe, something that is contrary to what most people believe."[10]

When a person fails to believe even some of the simple or easy truths, this means that some of the basic, fundamental cells in their network of beliefs are turned "Off." Since they do not believe these simple truths, vast segments of their spreadsheet are also turned "Off." Their spreadsheet is darkened with unbelief because they don't even believe some of the simple, foundation-

[10] Wilkin, "Should We Rethink the Idea of Degrees of Faith?", 10.

al, basic truths of life or Christianity. They have little faith, that is, an undeveloped and unexamined spreadsheet of beliefs. On such a spreadsheet of faith, most of the basic truths are still turned "Off."

On the other hand, there are some people who have great faith. These are those people who are persuaded or convinced of some difficult things to believe. People who have great faith believe truths and ideas that relatively few people understand and believe. There are truths in Scripture, life, and theology that are hard to believe, but people with great faith believe them. Such ideas often take great thought, insight, understanding, research, investigation, or deep spiritual experiences in order to believe them. When people come to believe these things, they believe something that few others believe, and can therefore be described as having great faith. Vast segments of their spreadsheet of beliefs are lit up with the light of the truth of God.

Some examples from Scripture might be helpful. There are numerous truths from Scripture that are easy to believe. These might include the statements that "A man named Jesus existed" or that "I am a sinner." Almost everybody believes these, including most non-Christians. Yet people with little faith do not even understand or believe these truths. People with little faith have trouble believing some of the simple, elementary, and introductory truths of Scripture, such as "God is love" or "Jesus gives eternal life to anyone who believes in Him for it." It is a telling fact of the condition of faith in our churches when most Christians don't truly believe these things. As simple as these truths are, many do not believe them.

However, there are other truths in Scripture which are hard to believe. People who believe these difficult truths have great faith. For example, it is difficult to believe that "God will supply all of your needs according to His riches in glory" (Php 4:19). Frankly, since I often worry about tomorrow, this means that I don't believe this promise. I don't believe that God will supply all my needs, and often find myself trying to supply for my own needs. So this means I don't yet believe this statement. But those who have great faith believe it.[11]

So great faith and little faith have nothing to do with the amount of faith one has, or the percentage to which one believes a particular fact. Faith does not come in degrees or amounts. Therefore, we must not feel bad when we discover we have little faith. Instead, if we discover that we have little faith, we must seek to learn, study, and grow in our relationship with God so that we can turn "On" more cells in our spreadsheet of faith, thereby gaining great faith.

In the Gospels, the people of Israel and Jesus' own disciples are often chided for having little faith. Ironically, though they prided themselves in being men and

---

[11] Some of these ideas are drawn from my article, "Now That's Faith!" http://faithalone.org/magazine/y2008/faith.html Last accessed December 19, 2018.

women of faith as descendants of the father of faith, Abraham, they were chastised over and over for their lack of faith.

In these instances, note that that while Jesus did speak of their little faith, He often turned around and praised the Roman guards and Gentiles for their great faith. Yet He never once invited people to have "more faith." Why not? Because, as we have already seen, faith does not come in percentages or degrees. We do not have "faith containers" in our souls which fill up bit by bit until they overflow when our faith is great. Faith does not work like that. Scripture invites us to believe more truths, and provides us with the evidence to do so, but we are not called or challenged to grow more faith. The reason for this is because of the fourth truth about faith.

4. WE CANNOT CHOOSE TO BELIEVE ANYTHING

Since faith occurs when we are persuaded or convinced by the evidence presented to us, this means that we cannot choose to believe. Belief, or faith, is not a decision we make.[12] Faith is something that happens to us when presented with convincing and persuasive arguments or experiences in favor of the belief. Faith occurs when we are persuaded about the truth of something. Each truth we come to believe is formed by building upon other

[12] Wilkin, *Confident in Christ*, 6.

truths we already believe. But the level of verification required can change from person to person.

For example, some people might not be able to believe certain truths until they verify it with their own eyes. Others, however, might be able to believe that same fact simply on the word or testimony of someone they trust. All historical facts are of this second type. Any historical fact can only be believed on the testimony of others. But with other types of facts, we might come to faith through reason, logic, and the weight of argumentation.

Occasionally, we might even come to believe something despite our desire to not believe it. If a father was told that his son was a mass-murderer, the father would not want to believe it, and would likely not believe it. But if this father sat through the trial of his son, and saw the weight of evidence, and maybe even heard the confession of his son to these crimes, the father would be forced to believe what he did not want to believe. In such an instance, the father did not choose to believe, but was persuaded or convinced by the evidence presented, and came to believe something he did not wish to be true.

Or consider once again the "Sky is blue" illustration. If you had simply told me that the sky was violet, I would not have believed it. But once I was presented with the evidence, I was persuaded to believe that the sky is violet. This belief even goes against what I see with my own eyes. Although I *see* that the sky is blue, I know that something is going on with the light receptors in my eyes that causes it to appear blue, when in fact it is violet. So despite all the *visible* evidence, the scientific facts persuaded me to believe that the sky is violet. I did not choose to believe that the sky is violet; I was persuaded by the evidence.

This is how faith works. Every fact we believe, we believe because we are persuaded by the evidence. We did not choose to believe or make a decision to believe. Belief happens to us as the evidence is presented before us.

> Belief is not something we conjure up by strength of will. The key to believing something is the proof in favor of it. Faith is not really a choice. You don't choose to believe anything. Either you believe that two plus two equals four, or you don't. You can't *choose* to believe it. When the evidence that something is true persuades people, they believe it. When the evidence is insufficient, people don't believe it. … Therefore, faith is not a decision. It is the conviction that something is true.[13]

Since we cannot choose to believe anything, but are only persuaded by the evidence presented to us, we can never judge or condemn someone for their lack of faith on a particular topic or idea. All we can do is present evidence to them and engage with them in conversa-

---

[13] Cf. Bob Wilkin, *The Ten Most Misunderstood Words in the Bible* (Denton, TX: GES, 2012), 20.

tions about what they believe. The same is true for our own beliefs. We cannot feel proud of our beliefs, nor can we feel guilty about things we don't believe. All we can do is think, reason, discuss, learn, and investigate the truth. As we do this, faith will blossom in us as we come to know, understand, and agree with the various propositions that we learn. Here is what Dallas Willard writes about this process:

> Our beliefs ... cannot be changed by choice. We cannot just choose to have different beliefs ... But we do have some liberty to take in different ideas and information and to think about things in different ways. We can choose to take in the Word of God, and when we do that, [our] beliefs ... will be steadily pulled in a godly direction.

> We never *choose* to believe, and we must not try to get ourselves or others to choose to believe. ... We can try to understand and try to help others to understand. And beyond that—God must work. Once we understand this and stop trying to get people to choose to believe or to do things they really don't believe, He will certainly work as we do our part.[14]

C. S. Lewis agrees. In many of his letters to various people, Lewis wrote about how he became a Christian. He writes that was persuaded against his will about the existence of God and the truth of Christianity. He did

[14] Dallas Willard, *Renovation of the Heart* (Colorado Springs: NavPress, 2012), 248.

not choose to believe or even want to believe, but was persuaded to believe by the evidence.

As people faced similar experiences of faith in their own life, Lewis wrote to them with counsel that just as they cannot fight faith, so also, they cannot force it. Faith happens to us as the light of God shines in our life. This does not mean we have no responsibility in faith, but that we must respond positively to the revelation God has given to us so that we can receive more revelation from Him. Here are a few examples of what Lewis wrote to various people:

> If you think [Christianity] is false you needn't bother about all the things in it that seem terrible. If you decide it is true, you needn't worry about not having faith, for apparently you have.[15]

> If you don't think [Christianity] is true why do you want to believe it? If you do think it is true, then you believe it already.[16]

> No one can make himself believe anything and the effort does harm. Nor make himself feel anything, and that effort also does harm. What is under our own control is action and intellectual inquiry. Stick to that.[17]

[15] C. S. Lewis, *Yours, Jack: Spiritual Direction from C. S. Lewis* (New York: HarperCollins, 2008), 91.

[16] Ibid., 125.

[17] Ibid., 126.

C. S. Lewis is right. We cannot force ourselves to believe something. But at the same time, nor can we fight it. Faith happens to us when we are persuaded by the evidence presented. Of course, faith is not always the result of evidence and logic, but can also come through experience and emotions. While facts, logic, and reason can lead to faith, so also can experience, relationships, and revelation. Even hope and trust, which are not themselves faith, can be transformed into faith. Even faith itself can lead to greater faith, for once we believe some things about God, it becomes easier to believe other things. Divine revelation itself can lead us to believe things about God, ourselves, and eternity which we may not have believed otherwise (cf. Rom 10:17).

Note that to some degree, our beliefs depend on the reliability of the person who made a particular truth claim to us. When we believe, we not only believe based on the evidence of the facts presented, but also on the reliability of the source of those facts. For example, I believe that $E=MC^2$ because I believe that Einstein was smart enough to figure it out. If a kindergarten student tells me that Einstein was wrong, I am not likely to believe him. We use reason and logic to judge what we hear, so that we are either persuaded or unpersuaded by the truth claims of other people. Because I have more trust in Einstein than a 6-year old when it comes to the Theory of Relativity, I believe what Einstein says. However, I am more likely to believe a six-year old than Einstein when it comes to the best tasting candy.

The spreadsheet analogy is of further aid in this regard. One cell the spreadsheet of beliefs contains the truth claim that $E=MC^2$. I believe this. But the truth of this cell is dependent upon another cell which says "Einstein was a genius." Based on what I have read and learned about him, I also believe this. There is another spreadsheet cell which says "Einstein was infallible." I do not believe this. However, even though I do not believe Einstein was infallible, I can be reasonably certain of many of the other truth claims from Einstein, as well as nearly all of the things he taught related to the Theory of Relativity, and so when it comes to the truth claim that $E=MC^2$, I am persuaded to believe it.

Do you see how this works? Faith is a persuasion or conviction that something is true. Some people require more persuasion; some less. Some truth claims require more reasoning; some less. But in all cases, we cannot choose to believe something that we do not think is true. Furthermore, in no case does God invite us to turn off our brains and "just believe it." Quite to the contrary, God invites us to think and use reason to figure things out. God does not call us to turn off our minds. He gave us our minds for a reason ... which is reason.

We cannot, of course, always depend upon reason to properly guide us. It is as John Donne once wrote in "Holy Sonnet XIV":

> *I, like an usurp'd town, to another due,*
> *Labor to admit you, but O, to no end.*
> *Reason, your viceroy in me, me should defend,*
> *But is captive, and proves weak or untrue.*

Reason and logic are helpful in the development of faith, but reason can often lead us astray, partly because we are not omniscient, as God is. If we had all facts and knowledge, then our reason and logic would be infallible as well. But since there are great chasms of ignorance in our understanding of all things, our reason often leads us astray.

But even though reason is not entirely reasonable, God has not left us to our own devices. Due to the unreliability of reason, God has given us numerous allies to help reason in our quest for truth. God does not leave us alone in this process to figure things out on our own.

Along with Scripture and other humans to help guide our reasoning process, God has also given Himself in the person and work of the Holy Spirit. Prior to conversion, the Holy Spirit works upon the minds of unbelievers to convict them that they are sinners, that they need righteousness in order to get to receive eternal life, and that judgment is coming (John 16:8-11). This convicting work of the Holy Spirit involves persuading unbelievers to believe things that they did not previously believe. Even after we become Christians, the teaching and illuminating work of the Holy Spirit continues. Through Scripture, by the Spirit, and in the midst of life experiences and human relationships, God works to continually "renew our minds" (Rom 12:1-2; cf. 10:17) so that we come to know, understand, and believe the truth.[18]

In light of this fact that we cannot choose to believe or change our beliefs with a simple act of the will, but are instead persuaded to believe by the evidence presented to us, we see the fifth and final truth about faith.

5. WHEN A BELIEF CHANGES, OTHER BELIEFS ALSO CHANGE

This final insight about how faith works has already been mentioned numerous times in this chapter. Since our system of beliefs is like a giant spreadsheet of interconnected cells, it makes perfect sense that a change in one belief will cause a change in numerous other beliefs as well. When we come to believe something that we previously did not, this new belief has a cascading effect throughout our spreadsheet of beliefs so that we stop believing some things and start believing others. Note, however, that when a belief changes, we do not stop believing everything else on the spreadsheet. Our network of beliefs do not all stand or fall together. When one belief changes, it simply causes several other beliefs

---

[18] Gordon Clark, *Faith and Saving Faith* (Jefferson, MD: Trinity, 1983), 107. Cf. Also Zane Hodges, "The New Puritanism, Part 2" *JOTGES* 6:11 (Autumn 1993), http://www.faithalone.org/journal/1993ii/J11-93b.htm. Last Accessed January 29, 2004.

to change as well, which in turn causes more beliefs to change. So yes, these changes can sometimes occur on a large scale, but these changes are usually for best.

For example, on everybody's spreadsheet of beliefs there is a cell which says, "God exists." For some people, this cell is switched "Off" because they don't believe it is true. Others are uncertain about whether or not this statement is true. For them, the cell is also "Off." But for many people, myself included, this cell is switched "On" because we believe it to be true.

But this belief is not based on an illogical "blind leap of faith" (a terrible term!) into the dark void. This belief in the existence of God is based on a large number of beliefs that reside in other cells. Among these other cells are the beliefs that "Matter exists," "Matter cannot come from nothing," "Matter is not eternal," and "Matter had to have been 'created' by something outside of matter." These sorts of beliefs are turned "On" in my spreadsheet, and ultimately, are some of the beliefs that lead me to believe that "God exists." When taken as a belief *all by itself*, I could never believe that "God exists." But since this belief is based on other reasonable beliefs, I am able to state with full confidence that "God exists."

Many people think that believing in the existence of God is a blind leap of faith. But it isn't. People who believe that God exists maybe have not thought through all the rational arguments for the existence of God, but the only way that anyone comes to believe that God exists is by being persuaded of this truth in some way. Their new belief in the existence of God was due to some preliminary, foundational beliefs also changing. Maybe they heard some of the logical and rational arguments for the existence of God. Maybe they were persuaded by a personal experience, or the experience of someone else whom they trust. Maybe they simply excluded all other possibilities, and came to realize that a belief in the existence of God was the only remaining and reasonable possibility.

But regardless of how a person comes to believe in the existence of God, as soon as they believe this, numerous other beliefs will also start to change. They will eventually realize that since God exists, then God has authority (to some degree) over humans. And when they come to realize this, they will also come to believe that God would seek to exert that authority by telling us how to live our lives. This leads to a belief in some form of divine revelation from God.

Do you see how one belief starts to cascade and ripple through the rest of the spreadsheet of beliefs? This cascading ripple of changing beliefs is not instantaneous, but often takes some time to fully work its way through the spreadsheet. Sometimes this process can take an entire lifetime.

The process of changing beliefs can also be stopped, short-circuited, and even reversed. If a person comes to believe in the existence of God, but then someone else comes along and starts to challenge the various foundational beliefs that support the idea of the existence of God, this challenge might cause the person's faith in God to unravel and reverse. If a person recognizes that their feelings cannot always be trusted, that sometimes their pastor and parents are wrong, and that the Bible seems to contain some apparent contradictions about God (which I think can be rationally explained), then the person might end up turning their "God exists" cell from "On" back to "Off." Understandably, this change will then have further ripple effects throughout the system of beliefs.

Ideally, we should personally investigate the truth claim of every single cell in the entire spreadsheet of knowledge. Yet since there are an infinite number of truth claims, this exercise is humanly impossible. We simply do not have the time, ability, or experience to analyze the vast majority of the possible truth claims.

So what are we to do? Well, we humans tend to investigate the ones that are interesting to us, and then accept or reject the rest based on the input of others. To use Einstein again, I don't have the time, ability, or necessary knowledge to analyze the truth claim that $E=MC^2$, but I still believe that this statement is true. Why do I believe it if I haven't really investigated it for myself? I believe it because I believe in Einstein (and other physicists who also believe it). I believe they have studied this truth claim, have understood it, and have agreed that it is true. Therefore, because I trust their judgment on this matter, I believe that $E=MC^2$.

The same exact thing happens with the majority of the cells in our Excel Spreadsheet of beliefs. Most of the things we believe, we believe because someone else told us to believe them. Some of these claims we later investigate for ourselves, and either confirm or correct them, but the vast majority we simply accept based on the reliability and trustworthiness of the one who initially taught them to us. God, of course, is the most reliable teacher of truth, and so anything He says can be believed. So we should always be open to God showing up in our life to challenge some of what we believe, even if it is the beliefs that we hold dear.

Nevertheless, the potential back-and-forth tidal wave of shifting beliefs can cause some fear and frustration in the minds of those who experience it. It can indeed feel like a house of cards tumbling down around you. This is terrifying for those who thought their "house of cards" was really a true house. When someone thinks that their beliefs are the foundation to all that is true and right, and then this foundation starts to shake and crumble, it can be very disconcerting. Some people will retreat from all questions and investigations just so that they can avoid this feeling.

But I hope that as you come to understand how faith works, you can learn to enjoy and anticipate this feeling of having the rug pulled out from beneath you. If you can view this experience as the most exhilarating ride of life, rather than as the destruction of everything you have worked so hard to build, then the rippling changes of beliefs will not be something to fear, but to enjoy.

For those are terrified of changing their beliefs, or believing something wrong, I would say that the one belief which provides peace of mind and stability of spirit throughout all these shifting tides is the belief that Jesus will never let you go. If you do not know that you are safe and secure in the arms of Jesus for all eternity, then yes, the potential ramifications of changing your beliefs will be terrifying. But do not be terrified. Instead, seek to learn that God loves you perfectly, and perfect love casts out fear. He will never stop loving you, nor will He ever let you go.[19] This belief is a foundational and core belief for life as a Christian. Without it, I do not see how you can safely investigate your faith or navigate this life.

But when you are able to stand firm on the solid rock of Jesus Christ, then no amount of shifting beliefs can shake you. Instead, you can howl into the wind and laugh at the driving rain as you stand side-by-side with Jesus. Embrace the change, for that is where the thrill of the Christian life truly resides.

---

[19] I invite you to read my book, *The Gospel According to Scripture* (Dallas, OR: Redeeming Press, 2018), so that you might be persuaded and convinced (believe) that Jesus will never let you go.

CONCLUSION

As a result of this chapter, it is possible that you have changed your belief about belief. That is, you now likely believe something different about how faith works than you previously believed. If your understanding of faith has indeed changed, and you now believe something different about faith than you previously believed, this means that several other "cells" in your spreadsheet of beliefs have also likely changed (or are in the process of changing). You have likely stopped believing several false (but popular) misconceptions about faith. The next chapter considers several of these.

CHAPTER 3

SIX MISCONCEPTIONS ABOUT FAITH

There are many things that faith is not. Robert Wilkin summarizes some of these when he writes that faith is not "promising to serve God, praying, walking an aisle, being sorry for your sins, turning from your sins, inviting Jesus into your heart ... doing good works, or having heart faith."[1] Strangely, it is exactly these sorts of misconceptions that are quite popular in many streams of modern, evangelical Christianity.

When I teach others that "eternal life is freely given to anyone who simply believes in Jesus for it," it is not uncommon for someone in the room to object by saying, "So you believe that anyone who raises a hand or walks an aisle can be saved?" This sort of question often leads into a short discussion about the nature of faith and the definition of the word "saved."[2] I try to point

---

[1] Wilkin, *Confident in Christ*, 9.

[2] See my book, *The Gospel Dictionary* (Dallas, OR: Redeeming Press, Forthcoming).

out that faith is not the same thing as raising a hand, signing a card, walking an aisle, or saying a prayer. All such actions are works, and faith is not a work.

Similarly, the concept of faith is often portrayed with faulty illustrations.[3] This book began with the illustration of the wheelbarrow over Niagara Falls, but there are numerous other popular (and misleading) illustrations as well. Some people talk about faith as a chair in which you must sit if you are going to demonstrate your faith that the chair can hold you up. I have heard others teach that faith is like a rope off the side of a cliff to which you must cling for dear life. If you stop believing and let go of the rope you will plummet to your death on the rocks below. Then there is the illustrations of the airplane that needs two wings, both faith and works, before it can properly fly.

We could go on and on with many similar faulty illustrations. But let us just note for now that illustrations are not proofs of a concept. Rather, they are nothing more than pictures that the speaker or author uses to help others understand a concept. If the concept is inherently wrong, then the illustrations will also be wrong. And since many people falsely conflate the concepts of faith and works, thinking that the terms are identical, synonymous, or that faith always results in good works, this means that many illustrations of faith also include an element of works. They say "You have to hold on to

[3] Bob Wilkin, "Evangelistic Illustrations: The Good, The Bad, and the Ugly," GES Annual Conference Audio CD, 2003.

the rope ... you have to sit in the chair." But when we understand faith as it has been presented in this book, we are able to see that many of these illustrations about faith are wrong, and so also are the concept of faith that rest behind these illustrations.

So in this chapter we are going to consider several misconceptions about faith. Many of these misconceptions are quite popular and have led many Christians into bad theology and poor thinking about how we gain, keep, or prove that we have eternal life, as well as how to live the Christian life. Since faith is central to both types of life, we must rid ourselves of any misconceptions about faith we have if we are to live life as God wants and desires. The following chapter accomplishes this by looking at six misconceptions about faith.

FAITH IS NOT A BLIND LEAP

Every time I hear someone talk about faith as a blind leap, I think of the scene from "Indiana Jones and the Last Crusade" where the treasure map tells him to leap over a gaping crevice to get to the other side. But it is too far to jump. However, just before he turns back, he hears his dying father cry out, "Just believe!" So Indiana takes a deep breath, closes his eyes, clenches his hand over his chest to calm his beating heart, and then steps out into the void. Upon doing so, however, he discovers that there was a hidden bridge across the crevice, which had been painted to look exactly like the far side of the crevice. Now that he was on the bridge, his perspective had changed, and so he could see the bridge perfectly. He walks across and continues toward the treasure.

For many people this is how faith works. They think of faith as stepping out into the void and hoping that something catches them. This is why it is referred to as "blind faith" or "taking a leap of faith." Some even refer to this type of faith as "faith like a child," which apparently means that they don't need reason or logic to believe something, but instead "just believe it." The faith like a child passage (Matt 17:20) will be discussed in a later chapter, but for now, simply note that "faith like a child" is not an ignorant, uncomprehending leap into the great unknown. Similarly, there is no such thing as "blind faith" or a "leap of faith." By definition, it is impossible to accept unproven facts or to believe something you don't (at least partially) understand.

While it is true that different people require different levels of persuasion to believe certain truths, and while some people can believe things with very little evidence to support their belief, there is no such thing a completely blind leap of faith. When we believe something "blindly" we are actually basing that belief on a whole set of additional beliefs in the background. You might believe in the reliability of the person who told you what to believe, and since you believe in them, you believe what they say. Similarly, a person might not recognize

how their network of beliefs are related and interconnected, so their "blind leap of faith" appears to be an
unconscious logical step of faith, when in reality, it is
based on what is already believed.

Furthermore, nowhere does the Bible talk about anything related to blind faith or a leap of faith. Quite to
the contrary, the Bible invites us to use our minds, and
to engage in reasonable questioning with God about life
and faith (Isa 1:18). Jesus doesn't chide Thomas for not
believing that He is risen, but instead, provides the evidence Thomas needed to believe that Jesus has risen
from the dead (John 20:27). The Bereans are praised for
questioning what Paul taught and reasoning from the
Scriptures to see if they should believe what he said
(Acts 17:11). Paul even encourages the doubting Corinthians to corroborate his story of the resurrected Christ
with other living eye-witnesses (1 Cor 15). In all such
cases (and everywhere else in the Bible), no one is commanded or invited to take a leap of faith, but instead to
think, learn, question, study, discuss, and reason things
out so that they might believe.

Consider the scene once again from "Indiana Jones
and the Last Crusade." While it is true that he did not
know about the hidden bridge, he did know that the
treasure map in his hands had never led him astray. He
also saw the very clear picture in the treasure map of
what he was supposed to do, namely, step straight out
into the apparent void. Also, he knew that the word of

his father could be trusted. So for Indiana Jones, in this situation, these foundational beliefs logically led him to believe that if he stepped out into the chasm, he would somehow get across. He didn't know *how* he would get across, but he had enough reason to know (or believe) that it would work.

So the concept of blind faith is nothing more than a modern invention. And since it does not fit with any biblical perspective of faith, nor does it fit with how faith actually works, we must eradicate all thoughts about blind faith from our thinking and theology. Blind faith does not exist, and we must stop telling people to "Stop thinking and just believe!" Similarly, we must never say, "You're asking too many questions; you just have to experience God!" Such phrases and ideas cause non-believers to think that Christianity is little more than a fairy-tale to entertain people with weak minds. We must instead invite people to think, question, and doubt. We must tell them that if Christianity is true, then it can stand up to any and all questions.

And indeed it can. There are rational reasons to believe in Jesus, and rational arguments for the existence of God. While a person is not required or expected to know *all* of these explanations and arguments for anything they believe, they do need to know enough to be persuaded or convinced in their own mind of what they believe. If they do not know, then they do not believe. So-called "blind faith" is not faith at all, but is little more than wishful thinking, and does not have any place in Christian theology.

FAITH IS NOT "ALL OR NOTHING"

This misconception about faith was partly addressed in the previous chapter, but it is worth considering here as well. Some people think that when it comes to "believing in Christianity" you have to believe all of it or none of it. This is the "all or nothing" approach to faith. My Grandmother was a person who thought like this. Before she passed away, my Grandmother thought that since she could not believe that Methuselah lived to be 969 years old, this meant that she could not believe anything in the entire Bible.

Greg Boyd's "house of cards" analogy also fits within this misconception of faith. As he rightly pointed out, if someone thinks that the entire Christian faith stands or falls together, then whenever one particular facet of faith is challenged or changed, the entire house of cards comes tumbling down. This is a terrifying prospect for the Christians who hold the "All or Nothing" approach to faith, which is why so few Christians ask hard questions or investigate any ideas that might challenge their beliefs.

So the proper approach to faith is to recognize that while the various beliefs we can hold are all interconnected and related to each other in a vast network, they do not all stand or fall together. Faith is not a house of cards. Yes, changing one belief can cause a cascading change to ripple through numerous other beliefs, but the end result of this process is a stronger set of beliefs that can now stand up against further questions and stronger storms of life. And while it can be disconcerting and scary the first few times these largescale changes occur, if you remember that Jesus will never let you go, then you will start to enjoy the thrill of the roller-coaster ride of faith, rather than dread any new change that comes along.

If I were able to have a conversation with my Grandmother today, I would praise her for questioning the idea that Methuselah lived to be 969. After all, all questions are good questions. I would even tell her that it is completely okay if she never believed this particular historical claim. But I would then encourage her to move past this difficult idea from Scripture, and consider some of the more central truth claims from the Bible, such as some of the claims about Jesus as found in the Gospels. And if she wasn't yet able to believe most of these either, that also would be okay. We would keep reading, discussing, questioning, and learning, as we built upon whatever truths she could believe. Faith is not "all or nothing" but is an adventure in which you move from what you know into the great unknown, so that some of the other hidden gems of God and treasures of truth might be discovered and enjoyed.

FAITH IS NOT HOPE

Often, when people use the word "believe," they use it in a way that confuses it with hope. Though someone might say they believe the Bears will win the Super Bowl this year, they know, as does everyone else, that their belief is little more than hope. You even sometimes hear people say "I believe I will win the lottery!" In this case, the word "believe" doesn't even rise to the level of hope, but is nothing more than fanciful thinking. Yet people might also say "I hope the Bears win the Super Bowl" or "I hope I win the lottery" and mean essentially the same thing as when the word "believe" was used. Since "believe" and "hope" can be used interchangeably to refer to a wish or desire, it makes sense that English speakers confuse the two concepts.

Yet in Scripture, faith and hope are distinctly different. In 1 Corinthians 13:13, for example, Paul writes, "And now abide faith, hope, and love ... but the greatest of these is love." If faith and hope were the same, then Paul's statement would be nonsense. A similar idea is taught in Hebrews 11:1, which says, "Now faith is the substance of things hoped for ..." Again, if faith and hope are the same, then the author is saying that belief is the substance of things believed for. This makes no sense. So while it is true that faith and hope are intimately connected in Scripture, they are not synonymous terms.

In biblical usage, what do the two words mean and how are they connected? We have already seen that faith is the confidence, persuasion, or conviction that something is true. Faith is (as will be discussed further below) the mental assent to a factual statement. Biblical hope is built upon the foundation of faith. Unlike modern usage where hope is wishful thinking, biblical hope is the eager expectation of the future realization of a promise of God. Hope occurs when we believe what God has said about some future event, and then we look forward to it with earnest anticipation.

While faith is the knowledge that something is true, and this knowledge can involve past, present, or future events, hope is primarily concerned with the future. Hope involves that which has yet to happen, while faith can involve things in the past and present as well, including ideas and truths that have no reference to time at all. Hope, however, is always used in reference to a future event. Paul writes in Romans 8:24 that "hope that is seen is not hope; for why does one still hope for what he sees?" People do not hope for things they have already obtained or seen; hope is for things that will yet come to pass.

Since we believe what Jesus has said, and since we believe that Jesus will come again, we look forward to His return. That is, the return of Jesus is our blessed hope (Titus 1:2; 2:13; cf. John 14:3). Similarly, because we believe in Jesus and what He has said, all the promises of Scripture about our future life and blessings in eternity can be hoped for with an eager expectation (cf. 1 Tim 1:1). Hope, therefore, is a natural outcome of faith.

The relationship between faith and hope is illustrated by a young child who is told by her parents that they will be going to Disney Land later that year. Since she believes what her parents say, and since she believes that they can fulfill their promises to her, she looks forward to the trip to Disney Land. She hopes for it with eager anticipation. Her faith in her parents and what they say leads the child to hope.

So while faith and hope are complementary, they are not the same thing. We could say that while faith is grounded in facts and the reality of the past and present, hope is grounded in faith and expectations for the future. Faith leads to and gives birth to hope. This relationship between faith and hope also helps us understand the relationship between faith and trust.

FAITH IS NOT TRUST

Just as many people confuse and conflate faith and hope, so also, many people confuse and conflate faith and trust. In English, the two words are often used interchangeably. Banks remind their customers that their deposits have the "full faith and credit" of the United States Government. This means that the customer can trust the bank to keep and protect their money, and even if the bank closes down or declares bankruptcy, the US Government will make sure the customers get their money back. So just as "faith" and trust" are nearly identical in financial terminology, so also, the two words are nearly identical in the minds of many Christians. Most people do not see any real difference between the two statements "I trust Jesus" and "I believe Jesus."

Recall once again the example of the tightrope walker with the wheelbarrow. The tightrope walker asked the crowd if they believed he could walk across Niagara Falls while pushing somebody in a wheelbarrow. While they all enthusiastically shouted their support, when it came to actually trusting him with their own life, nobody wanted to get into the wheelbarrow. This illustration is sometimes presented as evidence that faith is not truly faith unless it includes trust.

But what this illustration *actually* proves is that there is a great difference between faith and trust. The people truly believed he could walk across Niagara Falls on a tightrope while pushing someone in a wheelbarrow. In fact, it is also quite likely that many people also believed he could do it with them in the wheelbarrow. But they did not believe he could do it *every single time.* They did not trust him to be 100% without mistake or error, nor did they trust themselves to be able to sit still while in wheelbarrow. So while they did believe, they did not fully trust. This lack of trust does not show a lack of belief, but instead reveals a key distinction between faith and trust.

Since faith is a mental assent in a proposition or a conviction and persuasion that something is true, trust is a particular *type* of belief. Trust is a belief in the strength, reliability, or dependability of someone or something. Not all beliefs are trusts, but all trusts are beliefs. Furthermore, while there are no degrees to faith (you cannot 99% believe something), there can be degrees of trust. I know that this can be confusing, for I just stated that trust is a form of belief, but a look back at the illustration of a giant Excel spreadsheet of beliefs helps clarify the difference between trust and belief.

On everybody's spreadsheet of beliefs are many thousands of statements about trust. For example, one cell says "I trust everything my parents taught me." Probably nobody (except very young children) would agree with that truth claim. For most people, this cell is turned "Off." Therefore, almost nobody believes this statement. However, there is another cell that says, "I trust a lot of what my parents taught me." More people are likely to agree with this, and so for them, this cell is turned "On." Some people, however, had terrible parents, and so they don't have either one of these two previous cells turned "On." Instead, they have a cell turned "On" which says, "I trust almost nothing my parents taught me."

So each statement resides in a separate cell on the spreadsheet of beliefs, but each cell contains a statement about the level of trust, or amount of trust, that someone has in another person. And depending on which cell is turned "On," this helps determine which other cells are turned "On" as well. Those who have more trust in their parents will therefore believe more of the truth claims they learned from their parents. Those who have less trust in their parents will believe less of what their parents taught. In this way, while belief in a particular factual statement is either "On" or "Off," the factual statement itself can have varying degrees of actuality.

To take this analogy a bit further, there is another cell on everyone's spreadsheet which says, "I 100% trust God to tell the truth." If a person believes this, then they know that God's words can always be trusted, and therefore, believed. A bit of careful thinking, however, reveals that while God can be trusted to always tell the truth, we humans cannot be trusted to always accurately understand what God has said. There is a vast difference between the statement "I 100% trust God to tell the truth" and "I 100% trust me to understand what God has said." Personally, I believe the first but not the second.

This distinction is similar to what we saw with the wheelbarrow story. While the crowed believed that the man *could* take someone across in the wheelbarrow, they did not believe that he *always* would. Instead, they believed with certainty that eventually, something would happen which would cause the man and a person in the wheelbarrow to plummet to their death below. Maybe it would be the person in the wheelbarrow who causes this fatal mistake. Nobody wanted to be in the wheelbarrow when that happened. So did they believe that he could do it? Yes. Did they fully 100% trust that he always would? No.

All of this reveals something critically important about the trust claims on our spreadsheet of beliefs. We have seen that while not every cell on the spreadsheet of beliefs is a trust claim, it is nevertheless true that every cell on the spreadsheet of beliefs is dependent or built upon several foundational trust claims. In other words, trust claims are foundational beliefs to nearly all of the cells on the spreadsheet. Early on in life, children trust their parents, and so their beliefs develop in accordance to what their parents teach them. As this trust in their parents grows or diminishes over time, the child's beliefs will also change.

All of this helps make better sense of what Scripture teaches about the relationship between trust and faith. The Greek word for trust is *peithō* and means "to have confidence" (cf. Matt 27:43; Mark 10:24; Luke 11:22; 18:9; 2 Cor 1:9; 10:7; Php 2:24; 3:4). This shows the connection between faith and trust, in that both are a form of confidence. Trust, however, is the confidence in the strength, reliability, or dependability of someone or something. The two concepts are related, but not identical.

For example, while Scripture everywhere calls us to believe in Jesus for eternal life (John 3:16; 5:24; 6:47; etc.), Scripture does not call us anywhere to trust in Jesus for eternal life.[4] Instead, since we trust what God has said, and Jesus is the perfect revelation of God, then we know we can believe everything Jesus says. Therefore, when Jesus offers eternal life to those who believe in Him for it, we know He is speaking the truth. The same thing is true for all the other teachings of Jesus. Since we trust Him, we can therefore believe in what He says. To put it another way, because we trust the character and truthfulness of Jesus, we are able to believe what He says. Belief in what Jesus says is based on the prior belief in the reliability and trustworthiness of Jesus.

If we think that belief and trust are identical, then statements like, "I believe what He says because I trust Him" would simply mean "I believe what He says because I believe Him," which is no reason at all. If we believe someone simply because we believe them, then our belief has no firm foundation and no basis on which to stand. We can, however, believe what someone says because we have previously understood that the person is reliable and trustworthy. When we believe that some-

---

[4] Bob Wilkin, "The Subtle Redefinition of Faith via Trust," https://faithalone.org/blog/the-subtle-redefinition-of-faith-via-trust/ Last Accessed March 17, 2018.

one is reliable and knowledgeable in what they teach, then this trust leads us to also believe what they say.

This distinction between faith and trust is further seen by the fact that while we can trust a person, we cannot really "believe a person." We can believe *what a person says*, or believe factual statements *about a person*, but you can no more "believe a person" than you can weigh a color or smell a number.[5] So although we do often say that we "believe Jesus," this is just a shorthand way of saying that we "believe various factual propositions about Jesus as well as truth statements from Jesus."

In the end, the relationship between faith and trust can be summarized this way: Though trust is a type of faith, it is not synonymous with faith. Though all trust claims can be believed or not, not all faith claims are trust claims. Instead, what and who we trust is a major determining factor in what or who we believe. Trust, therefore, is a precondition, or foundational element, to many aspects of faith. Just as faith leads to hope, so also, trust leads to faith. Quite often, we believe what we believe because we trust the person who taught these beliefs to us.

One of the reasons it is important to clarify the connection between faith and trust is because in the minds of many, trust involves action. When people equate faith and trust by saying that the two terms are synony-

[5] See Shawn Lazar, "Is Faith Trust in a Person?" https://faithalone.org/blog/is-faith-trust-in-a-person/ Last Accessed March 17, 2018.

mous, they will usually also say that eternal life is not simply by faith *alone,* but also involves some sort of action on our part, such as submitting to the Lordship of Jesus, persevering in obedience, or committing our life to Christ. We are told that these sorts of actions are indicative of true trust.

This leads to serious problems. When faith is equated with trust, and then trust is defined to include works and human activity, then works become a condition for receiving eternal life. This is why it is essential to maintain the distinction between faith and trust as explained above, and also to remember that faith is not a work. Faith is never something we *do*, or that requires us to *do* something in order to prove that we truly have faith. It is to this concept we now turn.

FAITH IS NOT AN ACTION

Almost nobody in evangelical Christianity argues that faith is a good work that we *do* to receive eternal life. Rather, most argue that if a person truly believes, then they will have the good works to back up their belief, or to prove that they have *really* believed. They argue that true faith always results in good works. Logically, therefore, if a person does not have the necessary good works, then they do not have faith. I argue against this entire line of thought in my book, *The Gospel According to Scripture,* and so what appears below is little more than a summary of the arguments presented in that other volume.

Note that if true faith always leads to good works, then this logically means that good works are a necessary requirement to spend eternity with God. Imagine two people who both claim to have faith in Jesus for eternal life. According to the "faith always results in works idea," if only one of them has the good works which provides the evidence for faith, then only the one with the good works will spend eternity with God. Since the only difference between them is the presence of good works, this means that good works were the deciding factor on whether or not a person spends eternity with God. In this way of thinking, faith alone in Jesus Christ is not sufficient for an eternal relationship with God. Instead, good works decide a person's eternal destiny.

When this point is brought up, one common objection is that even "faith alone in Jesus Christ" involves works, because we invite people to believe in Jesus. If believing in Jesus is something people *do*, or if faith is a human action, then even the call to "believe in Jesus" is a call to good works. Some argue, therefore, that whether it is the "good work" of faith, or the good works of obedience, eternal life is always gained through some form of good works. If this is true, we should all stop arguing about the role of faith and works in gaining eternal life for the believer, and instead call all people to a life of faith and good works toward God.

But eternal life is not based on human good works or effort in any way, shape, or form. It can be shown from Scripture, logic, and experience that faith does not necessarily lead to works, nor is faith itself a work. Let us consider both ideas in turn.

Despite the claims of many, true and genuine beliefs do not always lead to behaviors that match these beliefs. Quite to the contrary, people often behave in ways that do not match their beliefs. A smoker may rightly believe that smoking is bad for them, but due to a nicotine addiction, they continue to smoke. Does their ongoing habit prove that they don't *actually* believe that smoking is bad? Of course not. Other factors are in play so that such a person genuinely believes one thing, but acts in a way that is contrary to their belief. Numerous other examples could be provided. One could almost argue that as a general rule, humans act in ways that are contrary to their beliefs. Therefore, while our actions do *sometimes* indicate what we believe, actions are never an infallible guide for determining what a person believes or does not believe. Faith does not necessarily lead to works that match a person's beliefs, nor do the presence (or absence) of works indicate what a person believes.

What then can be said about this idea that faith is a good work? While it is definitely good to believe the truth, this is quite different than saying that belief is a good *work*. As seen earlier in this book, faith is something that happens to us when we are persuaded or convinced by the truth. While faith is mental assent to a stated proposition (see the section below), faith is not an act of the will that we set out to achieve or accomplish. We cannot "choose" to believe, "make a decision" to believe, or force ourselves to believe. Instead, as we discover the truth about a particular topic, or as that topic is taught to us, we are persuaded to believe, sometimes against our will. Therefore, if we do not choose to believe something, then it cannot be said that faith is an action or a work that we *do*. Faith is passive. It is something that happens to us when we are presented with the evidence for or against a particular idea.

It is critically important to recognize that faith is not a work or an action that we humans perform, for if it was a work, or a human action, then humans would be working for or earning their eternal life. In other words, since eternal life is received through faith, then if faith is a work we would have to conclude that eternal life is received through human work and action. But Scripture everywhere teaches exactly the opposite. Indeed, Paul clearly states in Romans 4:5 that God's righteousness is given to those who *do not work,* but believe. If faith was a work, then Paul would be saying that God justifies those who do not work, but work.

Grant Hawley, in his book *The Guts of Grace*, writes this:

> Phrases like, "For by grace you have been saved through faith … not of works …" (Eph 2:8-9), and, "to him who

does not work but believes" (Rom 4:5), are complete nonsense, if works are part of the definition of the words faith and believe. If a woman at a wedding reception said, "The one who does not move, but dances, enjoys the reception," you would wonder if she had had too much to drink because moving is part of the definition of the word dances.[6]

It is impossible and contradictory to say that salvation is by grace through faith apart from works (Rom 4:4-5; Eph 2:8-9), but through a faith that includes works. There are no works in faith. The two are diametrically opposed. Faith is not a special sort of human work, nor is it a divine work in the heart of the unbeliever. Faith is not a work at all; it is the opposite of works. Just as we do not receive eternal life by faith *and* works, so also, we do not receive eternal life by faith *that is* a work. Just as faith cannot be part of the definition of works, so also, works cannot be part of the definition of faith. The two are not related in any way, but are polar opposites. Both faith and works, by definition, are mutually exclusive.

So the idea that faith is a work is "a theological fiction which cannot be supported from Scripture."[7] Eternal life is the free gift of God to anyone who believes in Jesus for it. Eternal life is not received by works of any kind. Faith is being persuaded or convinced that what

[6] Hawley, *The Guts of Grace*, 124.

[7] Kevin Butcher, "A Critique of The Gospel According to Jesus," *JOTGES* 2 (Spring 1989), 38.

God says is true. God gives eternal life to anyone who believes in Jesus for it. Because of all that God has done in history, through various forms of revelation, and by His Holy Spirit, people are able to believe in Jesus for eternal life. Though all are invited and called to believe in Jesus for eternal life, this faith does not mean we are working for eternal life or in any way earning eternal life from God.

FAITH IS NOT A GIFT

Even though we have just seen that faith is not a work, some teach that faith *is* a work, but that it is a work of God. They say that faith is a work of God performed in the heart or mind of a person. Another way of saying this is that faith is a gift from God to the heart of human beings. Those who hold to this view say that God gives faith to those whom He has chosen for eternal life. There are three reasons that some people teach that faith is a gift of God.

First, some believe that since unregenerate people are "dead in trespasses and sins" (Eph 2:1), and have had their minds darkened or blinded (cf. (Eph 4:18; 2 Cor 3:14),[8] they cannot do anything good, including believing in Jesus for eternal life. Those who hold to this view teach that if a person is going to believe in Jesus for

---

[8] Yes, I agree with what all of these passages are saying. I just do not agree with how some Christians understand and explain them.

eternal life (or even believe anything good and pleasing about God at all), they can only believe if God sovereignly bestowed up them the gift of faith.

Various texts are often referenced in defense of this idea (cf. Acts 5:31; 11:18; 13:48; 16:14; Rom 12:3; 1 Cor 12:8-9; Eph 2:8-9; Php 1:29; 2 Tim 2:25; 2 Pet 1:1). But in several of these, faith is not even mentioned (e.g., Acts 5:31; 11:18; 2 Tim 2:25), and the others can all be reasonably explained in the context. A few will be explained below, with several others in a later chapter.

Note, however, that this entire line of thought stems from thinking that faith is a good work. In other words, the idea that faith is a gift derives from the false idea that faith is somehow meritorious. After all, if faith is a work, then we *must* say that faith is a gift from God, for we cannot teach that humans are able to work for eternal life.

But as we learned above, faith is not a work; it is not meritorious. Faith is the opposite of works (Rom 4:4-5). Faith does not earn, achieve, or gain good standing with God in any way. Therefore, faith does not *need* to be a gift from God. People are persuaded about all sorts of things, and no such persuasion is ever considered to be a good work or a meritorious action, or a gift from God. So the faith to believe in Jesus is also *not* a gift from God.

The second reason that some people believe and teach that faith is a gift of God is because they confuse this idea with the biblical teaching about the "spiritual gift" of faith. Even though Paul does write about the gift of faith in 1 Corinthians 12:9, this is the spiritual gift of faith, and is not the same thing as the so-called "gift of faith" which some teach God gives to people before they can believe in Jesus for eternal life. Furthermore, Paul is quite clear that we all have different spiritual gifts (Rom 12:6). If everyone had to receive the "gift of faith" from God in order to receive eternal life (John 3:16; 5:24; 6:47), then this would mean that all Christians have the spiritual gift of faith, which Paul says we do not.

So what is the *spiritual gift* of faith? As I wrote in my book on the spiritual gifts, a person has the spiritual gift of faith when they firmly persuaded of God's power and promises to accomplish His will and purpose and to display such a confidence in Him that circumstances and obstacles do not shake that conviction (1 Cor 12:8-10; cf. Heb 11).[9] They know what they believe and why they believe it, and are able to inspire action in others based on their beliefs. Those with the gift of faith are often called upon to encourage others to step out in faith and follow God to accomplish seemingly impossible tasks. As with all the spiritual gifts, the spiritual gift of faith is for the edification and encouragement of others in this world.

Often, those with the spiritual gift of faith are able to lead others in the direction God wants them all to go,

[9] J. D. Myers, *What are the Spiritual Gifts?* (Dallas, OR: Redeeming Press, 2018).

even when the others do not believe. In a way, the spiritual gift of faith can serve as "proxy" faith for those who do not have it. There was a time in my life where I doubted almost everything I had formerly believed about God, church, and the Bible. I knew that God existed, but I doubted that He was good and loving. I doubted the power of God to work in our lives. I doubted that Jesus cared very much for me. I doubted that God heard our prayers or answered them. For a period of a few years, I entered into a deep depression, and believed that God had abandoned me, forsaken me, and His only interest in me was to play games with my life. I felt like a pawn on a divine chessboard of life.

But during this time, my wife, Wendy, never stopped believing in the goodness and love of God. And while I was unable to believe, I saw her faith and was inspired by it to not completely give up on God. Though I did not believe that God was good, I saw that she believed this, and her faith served as a guiding light for my faltering faith. Though I had trouble believing much of anything good about God, I did believe in my wife, and what she knew to be true about God. Her unwavering faith eventually brought me back to faith as well. Of course, my beliefs were significantly altered and changed during this time of questions and doubt, but ultimately, my wife's spiritual gift of faith led me back to faith as well.

This is how the spiritual gift of faith works. It is not about God mystically opening up a person's mind to believe certain things that others cannot. Nor is it about some people believing more firmly, or more strongly, than others, for once again, there are no degrees to faith. Such a person might believe a larger number of difficult truths than others, which means they would have "great faith," but God did not "flip a switch" in their mind so that they believed these things.[10] Yes, God might present various truths to a particular person at a particular time, knowing that the presentation of these truths *at that time* will lead a person to believe, but this is not the same thing as God giving the gift of faith to this person. The timing and presentation of truths to a person might be a sovereign act of God, but the giving of faith *itself* is not.

So people believe difficult truths in the same way that anybody is persuaded to believe: the truths are taught to them and they are persuaded to believe based on the evidence presented to them. When they believe these difficult truths, they have "great faith." But that itself is not the spiritual gift of faith. The spiritual gift of faith is when God enables a person who already has "great faith" to lead and inspire others to accomplish

---

[10] Some do teach that the spiritual gift of faith is the divinely-bestowed ability to easily believe some of the more difficult truths about God, Jesus, and Scripture, but I have difficulty finding evidence for this idea in Scripture.

great tasks, and to encourage others who are struggling with their faith.

Therefore, in light of all this, we can see that the spiritual gift of faith to some Christians for the edification of others is not the same thing as God giving faith to all Christians so that they can believe in Jesus for eternal life. So biblical passages about the spiritual gift of faith cannot be used to support the idea that God gives faith to unregenerate people so they can believe.

The third reason that some people think faith is a gift from God is because of what Paul seems to say in Ephesians 2:8. He writes, "For by grace you have been saved through faith, and that not of yourselves, it is the gift of God." Some people see the phrase "and *that* not of yourselves, *it* is the gift of God" as referring back to the word "faith." They read Ephesians 2:8 this way: "For by grace you have been saved through faith, and faith is not of yourselves, faith is the gift of God."

There are numerous problems with this approach to Ephesians 2:8, the greatest being that it reveals a complete disregard for the Greek text. Greek words have gender: masculine, feminine, and neuter. When relative pronouns (such as "that" and "it") are used to refer back to a noun, they always agree with the gender of the noun. The word "faith" in Greek is feminine. Therefore, if Paul was intending to say that faith is not of ourselves, but faith is a gift of God, he would have used a feminine relative pronoun for the word "that" (the word "it" is not actually in the Greek).

But the word "that" is not feminine; it is neuter. Therefore, it is impossible for Paul to be thinking about "faith" when he wrote "and that is not of yourselves, it is the gift of God." So what was Paul referring to, if not to faith? Scholars have proposed various solutions, but the best solution is to see that the gift of God is the entire "salvation package" that Paul is writing about in Ephesians 2:1-22. Paul is teaching that humanity suffered under the problem of sin which we could not solve on our own, and so God stepped in to reveal the problem to us and show us the way out. This is the gift of God. If we believe in what God has shown, and live in light of it, we will be saved from the problem that has plagued humanity since the foundation of the world.[11] So Ephesians 2:8 does not teach that faith is the gift of God.

So we have seen the three main reasons that people think that faith is a gift from God. Let us now briefly consider six reasons we know that faith is *not* a gift from God. Many of these are drawn from an excellent article titled "Is Faith a Gift from God or a Human Exercise?" by René Lopez.[12]

---

[11] Note that in this context, "salvation" is not about going to heaven when we die, but is instead about living like Jesus in this life. In Ephesians 2, "salvation" is deliverance from the enmity that existed between humans so that we can live in in peace and unity with others instead.

[12] René Lopez, "Is Faith a Gift from God or a Human Exercise?" *Bibliotheca Sacra 164* (July–September 2007): 266-274.

First, Lopez points out that the idea that faith is a gift from God confuses the gift of eternal life from God with the instrumentality of faith, by which that gift is received. In other words, God does indeed give a gift to humans, but this gift is eternal life; not faith. Human receive the gift of eternal life through faith. To say that God gives the gift of faith as well is to confuse the gift itself with the receiving of the gift.

Second, Lopez says that "If God divinely imparts faith, then human responsibility is nullified."[13] In other words, if God is the one who sovereignly bestows faith upon a person, then no person can be held responsible by God for their lack of faith. If we receive eternal life by faith in Jesus, but nobody is able to believe unless God gives them the gift of faith, then God also cannot hold people responsible for not believing. If faith is a gift of God, then only God is responsible for people not having faith, and therefore, God has no basis on which to judge people for failing to believe.

Third, although the Bible calls people to believe in Jesus for eternal life, Lopez points out that if faith is a gift, then people should not be called to believe in Jesus (for they cannot). Instead, they should be called to pray and plead with God that He might regenerate them and give them the gift of faith. Strangely, these indeed *are*

http://www.dts.edu/download/publications/bibliotheca/BibSac-Lopez-IsFaithAGiftfromGodoraHumanExercise.pdf Last Accessed July 13, 2014.

[13] Lopez, "Is Faith a Gift From God or a Human Exercise?" 275.

works, and so if a person cannot believe on their own, but can only pray and plead with God to give them faith so that they might receive eternal life, we have now brought human works and effort back into the equation. Eternal life is no longer by faith alone, but is gained by praying and pleading with God for the gift of faith.

Thankfully, God does not call anyone to pray and plead that He might give them faith so that they might receive eternal life. To the contrary, God invites and calls all people to simply believe in Jesus. Although there are numerous calls throughout Scripture for people to believe in Jesus for eternal life (John 3:16, 36; 5:24; 6:47; etc.), there is not only place in Scripture where people are invited to hope and pray to God for regeneration (John 3:16; 5:24; 6:47). And when people believe, this faith is ascribed to humans, not to God (Matt 9:2, 22, 28-29; 10:52; Luke 7:50; 8:50; 17:19; 18:42; etc.)[14]

The fourth reason faith is not a gift from God is related to sanctification. If faith is the automatic gift of God to those whom He sovereignly regenerates, then it only makes sense that God also automatically and sovereignly guarantees that such people are sanctified in holiness and obedience. Indeed, this is what some theologians actually teach. But such a belief cannot be defended from Scripture, reason, or experience. The Bible is writ-

[14] C. Gordon Olson, *Beyond Calvinism and Arminianism: An Inductive Mediate Theology of Salvation* (Cedar Knolls, N.J.: Global Gospel Publishers, 2002), 225.

ten, not to tell us to just sit back and wait for God to sovereignly sanctify us, but so that we might change our beliefs and behaviors to bring them into conformity to the person and work of Jesus Christ.

> If faith is a gift, then many commands in Scripture that exhort, command, prompt, and warn believers to live obediently become superfluous because the ultimate end of infused faith guarantees the sanctification of believers without their involvement.[15]

The fifth reason that faith cannot be a gift from God is that such an idea raises too many questions from Scripture. For example, if faith is a gift from God, how could demonic activity restrict the faith of some (Luke 8:12; 2 Cor 4:4)? Why is it harder for some people to believe than others (cf. Titus 1:12-13)? What would be the point of the drawing work of the Holy Spirit (John 6:44; 12:32), or of evangelism and missions? Why was Jesus sometimes amazed at people's lack of faith (Matt 8:26; 14:31; 16:8)? None of these questions have good answers if faith is a gift of God.

Finally, if faith is a sovereign gift of God, God Himself appears to engage in favoritism. If God bestows faith on those whom He wants, why are there so many Christians in Europe and America, and so few in North Africa and the Middle East? Does God have something against the people in those neglected regions? On this

---

[15] Lopez, "Is Faith a Gift From God or a Human Exercise?" 275.

last question, missiologist C. Gordon Olson writes that if faith is a gift of God, then "one is forced to the conclusion that God is partial and loves Americans more than others."[16]

So we must conclude that faith is not a gift from God. There is no good reason to hold this idea. Therefore, since faith is not a gift from God, this means that anybody can believe in Jesus for eternal life. Even a little child. Of course, usually the more religious a person becomes, the harder it is for them to believe that God freely gives eternal life to anyone who simply and only believes in Him for it. This is why we can say that while faith in Jesus is simple, it is not easy. Most humans, especially those who are religious, want to add some of their own works and effort into the mix so that they can somehow earn eternal life from God. But they can't. Eternal life is a free gift, given to those who believe in Jesus for it. And some find this too hard to believe.

But once we break through the concepts of works-based righteousness and legalistic religion, faith in Jesus is quite simple. Anybody can believe in Him. God does not give some people the ability to believe in Jesus while denying this faith to others. No, faith is open and available to all. It is not a gift of God.[17] Each person is persuaded by the facts and ideas presented to them. And how is a person persuaded? If faith is not a gift, how

---

[16] Olson, *Beyond Calvinism and Arminianism*, 227.

[17] Cf. Wilkin, *The Ten Most Misunderstood Words*, 18-19.

does a person come to believe? It all begins with hearing the truth.

CONCLUSION

Since there are numerous ways that faith is presented in churches and Christian books, it is important to understand what faith is and is not. This chapter sought to clear up six of the more popular misconceptions about faith. Hopefully you now believe something new about belief! Hopefully you are becoming persuaded and convinced about how faith works and what faith is. But to further aid your thinking in this matter, the next chapter looks at five additional clarifications about faith. By understanding these five clarifications, you will come to further understand the nature of faith and how to know that you believe.

CHAPTER 4

FIVE CLARIFICATIONS ABOUT FAITH

I still remember when I got my first pair of glasses. Prior to getting glasses, I didn't know I was half blind. I just figured that the world was perpetually blurry for everyone. I discovered this was not the case in my early teens when I started taking Driver's Education. As we were driving around, the instructor told me to take a left on Davis Street. So as I approached the next intersection, I slowed way down and squinted at the little green sign so I could read what it said. It was Elm Street. So I sped up a bit until I reached the next intersection, and slowed down again to read the sign. It also was not Davis. Finally, I found Davis Street at the third intersection and made a left.

But the instructor noticed what I had done, and pointed to a big sign a couple hundred yards down the road. He said, "As we get near that sign, tell me when you can read it." We got nearer and nearer to the sign, and finally, when I was about fifty feet away, I read the sign to him. In reply, he said, "Pull over!" Then he explained that I was half blind, and he would not let me drive again until I got some glasses.

I went home and told my parents, and the next day I had an exam with the eye doctor. A few days later we went to pick up my new glasses. When I walked out of the doctor's office, I was amazed at what I saw. Trees were no longer green blobs; I could actually see individual leaves fluttering in the wind! I could actually see birds flying through the sky! A whole new world had opened up to me. It was the same world I had always lived in, but now I could actually see it. Rather than the world being filled with colorful blobs, I now saw things clearly and with precision.

The same exact thing can happen with faith. Many people grow up with fuzzy thinking about faith, and so they are never quite sure whether or not they actually believe. Many of them are trying to drive around without being able to clearly see the signs on the road. This is dangerous to them, and to others. It is important to know *what* you believe, *why* you believe it, and also *that* you believe. This chapter provides five clarifications about faith which will help you in all these areas. The five truths considered below will clear up your faith vision so that you can better see to understand Scripture and follow Jesus.

FAITH COMES BY HEARING

The first clarification is how we come to believe anything in the first place, and more specifically, how we come to believe in Jesus for eternal life. There are a large variety of factors behind every individual belief. Our beliefs are influenced by life experiences, education level (more is not always better), and how much trust we give to the authority figures who teach us. But in all cases, before we can believe something, we must first hear the idea or fact that we are invited to believe. We cannot believe something if we have never heard it.

This is why Paul writes in Romans 10:17 that "faith comes by hearing." This is true of all beliefs. You cannot believe that 2+2=4 until you first hear this mathematical fact. But hearing a fact is not the same thing as believing it. To believe it, we also need to understand the idea presented and agree that it is true. We come to agree with a fact when we are persuaded or convinced by the evidence presented in favor of it. A math teacher might show that two black marbles and two white marbles can come together to make four marbles. This sort of evidence helps children believe, agree, and become convinced that 2+2=4.

It is the same with spiritual beliefs. We cannot believe something about God or some spiritual truth about ourselves, until and unless we first hear the truth presented to us, along with various arguments and ideas that might help us believe this truth. According to Paul, the Word of God is a primary source of hearing these truths (Rom 10:17), but we must also not forget about the illuminating work of the Holy Spirit, or the influence of other people who pass on to us what they themselves believe. So before a person can believe in Jesus for eternal life, they must first hear the truth about eternal life in Jesus Christ, and also come to be persuaded or convinced about the truth of this offer by the evidence provided to them.

Nevertheless, some people criticize the idea that people are called and invited to believe in Jesus for eternal life. They say that this requires humans to take the first step toward God before He takes a step toward them. But nothing could be further from the truth. God has always taken the first step toward us. Indeed, God has taken the first trillion steps. He provided revelation through creation, conscience, Scripture, dreams, visions, and angelic messengers.

Furthermore, He sent prophets, missionaries, pastors, teachers, and evangelists to share the Gospel. He sent Jesus to fully reveal the true character and nature of God to humanity (John 14:9; Col 1:15; Heb 1:3). He sent the Holy Spirit to convict the world of sin, righteousness, and judgment, and uses the Holy Spirit to draw all people to Himself (John 6:44; 12: 32; 16:7-11; Acts 16:14, 29-30; 24:25). He created us with reason, intellect, emotions, and will. He constantly sends forth His grace and mercy upon all people (John 1:9; Titus

2:11). He forgives all sin, and is patient, loving, and kind to all.

These steps, and countless more specific steps in the life of each and every person, are the sorts of things God has done on our behalf to call each of us to believe in Jesus for eternal life. Human faith, then, is not the first step, or even the millionth step, in the process of coming to God or believing in Jesus for eternal life.

When it comes to the question of who has taken the first step, the answer is clearly God. In fact, there is no step that God could take which He has not already taken or will not take. If God *can* take a step to help us believe in Jesus; He will take it. But the one step which God cannot take is the step of forcing us to believe. God does not force Himself on anybody. Instead, people are able to believe in Jesus for eternal life because God has first done absolutely everything that is within His power, made everything available to us by His grace, and flung open the door to eternal life by His will. It is only because of this multitude of "first steps" by God toward us that anyone and everyone who wants to receive God's offer of eternal life may do so by simply and only believing in Jesus Christ for it.

This leads to the second clarification about faith. Since faith comes by hearing and reasonably considering the truth presented to us, this means that faith occurs within the human mind. In other words, faith is mental assent.

FAITH IS MENTAL ASSENT

Have you ever been accused of having "false faith" or "dead faith" because some person says that you only have an "intellectual faith"? I have. Now I agree (as my wife attests) that I have a tendency to overthink and overanalyze almost everything. This book might be a perfect example. Few people have attempted to dissect and analyze how faith works as I have done in this book. When I talked to my wife about the content of this book, she told me, "In an attempt to understand faith, it's like you're dissecting a cat to understand it. But you will enjoy and understand a cat much more if you simply pet it while it sits on your lap and purrs."

She has a point. But at the same time, all animal lovers need to be thankful for the animal analyzers who study and research animals, and even dissect them, for this is the only reason we have veterinarians and medicines that help keep our beloved pets alive. It is the same with faith. We must have people who think, analyze, study, read, research, and learn about what faith is and how faith works, for without such people, we would be tossed to and fro and carried about with every wind of doctrine (Eph 4:14).

And what we have so far seen about faith in this book is that faith truly does involve the mind. Faith uses the intellect; it *is* intellectual. Whether we realize it or not, all of our beliefs are based on reason, thinking, and analysis. Some people require more analysis than others, but nobody believes anything without first engaging in some sort of thought process about it. I challenge you to think of a single belief you have that you have not thought about in some way. You will not be able to find one, for you cannot believe anything without thinking about it intellectually to some degree or another.

Nevertheless, for some odd reason, people often discredit a "thinking" faith. Some argue that if you have to think about it, then it's not real faith. They say that people can miss heaven by 18 inches because they have a "head faith" instead of "heart faith." But no such terms or ideas are found in the Bible.[1] Others accuse people of having an "intellectual faith" which is only based on a "mental assent" to facts.

But isn't this exactly what faith *is*? Again, since faith occurs when we are convinced or persuaded that something is true, then this persuasion involves the mind. In other words, it is not wrong at all to say that faith is an intellectual assent to an idea or proposition, for that is exactly what faith *is*. Faith is being convinced or persuaded that a proposition is true. This is faith, and there is no other kind of faith. Faith is mental assent. Faith is intellectual.

In his book, *Beyond Doubt,* Shawn Lazar has an excellent summary of the types of things that can be believed.[2] He points out that you cannot believe physical

[1] Cf. Ibid., 11.

[2] Lazar, *Beyond Doubt*, 111-119.

objects, numbers, colors, or emotions, but you can believe in *statements* about such items. You can believe that a stone is heavy, but you cannot believe in the stone. You can believe that green is a combination of blue and yellow, but you cannot believe in green and yellow themselves. I believe that it makes me happy to drink coffee, but I do not believe in happiness itself. Furthermore, we can always believe (or not believe) promises and truth claims. If I promised to give you a $1 million, I hope you would not believe me. But since we know that Jesus never lies, we can believe anything and everything He says.

What this means is that beliefs are always based on propositions of things that might or might not be true. If we agree that a proposition is true, then we believe it. If we believe that a proposition is not true, then we do not believe it. If we are unsure about the truth of a proposition, then once again, we do not believe it. This means, therefore, that faith is propositional.[3] Sometimes people criticize others for having a "propositional faith" but in reality, there is no other kind. Faith is propositional. Faith is intellectual. Faith is mental assent.[4]

In fact, the word "assent" comes from the Latin word *assensus*, which can be translated as "assent, agree, approve, believe, or admit the truth of something." So mental assent is to admit or agree that something is true,

[3] Ibid., 117.

[4] Cf. Wilkin, *The Ten Most Misunderstood Words*, 10-11.

which is exactly the definition of "faith" that has been defended throughout this book. And of course, such "assent" takes place in your mind, which means that "mental assent" is a good synonym for faith.

> Believing is not something you do with your body, but with your mind. Someone tells you that "Canada is north of Mexico" and you *think* about what the proposition means. You weigh the evidence for and against it, you consider other possibilities, and ultimately, you come to a conclusion about whether it is true or false. You're either persuaded in your mind that the proposition is true, or you aren't. That's what faith is.[5]

The reason this is so important is because some people criticize the idea of "faith alone in Jesus Christ alone for eternal life" as a teaching that requires nothing more than "mental or intellectual assent" to some facts about Jesus." When I hear this, I am glad, for they have properly understood that faith is nothing more than mental assent. No works, trust, actions, or effort is involved. In order to believe something, you must understand what is being said, and you must agree, or assent, to the stated proposition.[6] Since belief is a persuasion or conviction that something is true based on the evidence provided, to "believe something" is another way of saying you "mentally assent" to it, that is, you understand and agree with it. So the next time someone accuses you

[5] Lazar, *Beyond Doubt*, 119.

[6] Cf. Ibid., 108.

of "just teaching mental assent" agree with them, for this is exactly right.

This is why the Bible includes so many facts and persuasive arguments about these facts. These historical facts and arguments are included so that we might be persuaded and convinced in our minds that what we read is true. God, through Scripture, wants us to give mental assent to what we read. When the biblical authors set out to teach what God wanted us to know, they did not simply lay out the facts and say "Just believe it!" Instead, along with the ideas we are to believe, they presented evidence.

Luke, for example, wrote that he was presenting a history of Jesus Christ (Luke 1:1-4) so that the reader could investigate these ideas and know with certainty that they were true. Similarly, when Paul set out to teach the Corinthian believers about the resurrection of Jesus, he didn't simply tell them to believe it, but instead presented rational arguments and eye-witness testimony about the resurrection so that they might be persuaded and convinced of what he wrote.

All the biblical authors (and therefore God Himself as the One who inspired the authors) wrote in a way that encourages people to think and reason about the ideas presented, so that they come to understand and agree with what is read. Those who engage with Scripture in this way are praised for doing so (cf. Acts 17:11).

So faith is mental assent. There is no other kind of faith than an intellectual faith. But if faith involves reason, investigation, and mental assent to the facts, then what does the Bible mean when it refers to childlike faith? This is the next clarification we consider.

FAITH LIKE A CHILD

Some Christians say that they don't need reasons or explanations for what they believe, because they have "faith like a child" or "childlike faith." When they say this, they mean that they don't ask questions about their beliefs, nor do they wonder if what they believe is true. Childlike faith is often described as a faith that does not doubt, question, or seek explanations; it just believes. But this is not childlike faith. So what is?

In seeking to understand what childlike faith *actually* is, let us look at four reasons why the lack of desire to ask questions is not "childlike faith."

First, while it is completely fine if a person does not *want* to ask questions about what they believe or seek answers about *why* they believe what they do, they should not look down upon those who do ask questions. Nor should they prohibit people from doing so. Some who claim to have "childlike faith" wear it as a badge of honor, seeming to indicate to others that their unquestioning faith is superior to those who ask questions and seek explanations.

For this reason, "childlike faith" could actually be called "arrogant faith" for those who claim to have it sometimes look down on those who require reason, logic, and explanations for what they believe. People who have this attitude will often say "I just believe the Bible" or "God says it, I believe it, that settles it." In reality, they don't "just believe the Bible." They believe a particular interpretation or explanation of the Bible, and often claim to "just believe the Bible" when someone comes along and presents a different perspective or explanation.

When faith is thought of as "blind faith" or a "leap into the void" in a way that does not require reason, logic, or explanation, those who are able to maintain this sort of faith sometimes have the tendency to look down on those who require reason, logic, and explanation for their beliefs. Of course, the opposite is also true. People who use reason and logic to support their beliefs often condemn those who don't for having an "ignorant and uneducated faith." This is not good either.

So if a person does not want to ask questions, there is no requirement to do so. Many people do not enjoy the "life of the mind" and should not be expected to engage in such practices. However, this preference should not be equated with childlike faith. Those who do not seek to dive deep into theology and seek answers to questions should not look down on those who do seek such answers as having a "lesser faith" (and *vice versa*). We will see below that both types of people can have childlike faith. So rather than say that a faith which does not question is "childlike faith" it might be better to simply call it an unquestioning faith.

This is the second reason that childlike faith cannot be equated with the lack of desire to ask questions. Childlike faith is not about the avoidance of questions, for children ask many, many questions. As any parent will tell you, the unrelenting barrage of questions from a two-year old can become quite exhausting. Therefore, it could easily be argued that true "childlike faith" is actually a faith that asks *lots* of questions. So the desire (or lack of desire) to ask questions has nothing to do with whether or not a person has childlike faith.

The third reason that a faith which does not ask question or seek explanations cannot be called "childlike faith" is because there are explanations and reasons for what a child believes … even if they themselves are not aware of what those reasons are. In other words, children do not believe anything without reason. The most common reason that children believe what they believe is because someone they trust told them what to believe. Children often simply believe whatever their parents and teachers tell them. This is not an unthinking faith, for the authority of the person who teaches is a factor that faith takes into consideration.

Something similar occurs whenever a person has a so-called "unquestioning faith." They do not believe without reason; they simply have not thought through what the reasons and explanations for their beliefs might be. They believe what a pastor or teacher taught them, or what seems to be the "plain reading" of Scripture (though careful, contextual studies of the text often reveal that the "plain reading" is not the best reading). There is nothing wrong with not knowing exactly *why* you have the beliefs you have, but a lack of understanding about *why* should not be confused with a lack of explanation. There *are* explanations for why you believe what you believe, even if you don't know what these explanations are.

And that's okay. Nobody has a complete explanation and understanding for why they believe what they believe. But everybody, over time, naturally and normally grows in their understanding and gains explanations for their beliefs. While initially, a belief might be gained because "I learned it in Kindergarten," this belief will either remain unquestioned and unchallenged throughout life, or it will be challenged and questioned. If it is challenged and questioned, the belief will either be supported and affirmed, or disproven and denied. But nobody's beliefs all stay the same throughout all of life. Instead, everybody matures and grows in what they think and believe. This is normal, natural, and just as God intended. Just as children grow and mature, so also does faith. This is the way God made humans, and this is the way God made faith.

Which brings up the fourth and final reason that unquestioning faith cannot be equated with childlike faith. And it is this: "childlike faith" is not found in the Bible. There is no such thing as biblical "childlike faith." When people refer to "childlike faith" or "faith like a child," they have in mind the sorts of things Jesus says in Matthew 18:3, Mark 10:14, and Luke 18:17, where He teaches that the kingdom of heaven belongs to little children. But in these passages, Jesus isn't talking about faith. In fact, He doesn't mention "faith" at all. Instead, Jesus is talking about entering the kingdom of heaven, and He encourages His listeners to humble themselves like a child and receive Him like a child (Matt 18:4-5; Mark 10:14) if they want to see the kingdom of heaven. In other words, there is something essential about the childlike perspective for the person who wants to see the kingdom of heaven.

But what is Jesus talking about? What is this childlike perspective that Jesus has in mind?

To begin with, it is critical to recognize that the kingdom of heaven is not eternal life. The phrase "see the kingdom of heaven" does not mean "go to heaven when you die." "Seeing the kingdom of heaven" is not the same thing as "going to heaven." These two concepts are not equivalent in the Bible. It is important that we recognize this, because Jesus says that seeing the kingdom of heaven requires humility. If seeing the kingdom of heaven was the same as going to heaven, then the good work of personal humility would be required for entrance into heaven after death. But eternal life is received by faith alone in Jesus Christ alone (John 3:16; 5:24; 6:47); not by living humbly before God. Good works are not required to gain entrance into heaven.

What then is the kingdom of heaven? In the Gospels, the phrase "kingdom of heaven" or "kingdom of God" refers to the rule and reign of God in our lives *now* on earth. It is about God's will being done on earth, as it is done in heaven (Matt 6:10). All the kingdom imagery and terminology in the Gospels is not about "leaving earth and going to heaven when we die" but about "heaven coming down to earth while we live." Seeing the kingdom of heaven is not about life after death, but about living and experiencing God's life in *this life* here and now.

This is what Jesus has in mind when He teaches about becoming like a little child. Experiencing the life of God in this life requires humility like a little child. In what way? Not by remaining ignorant, for God gave us Scripture so that we might learn, grow, mature, reason (Isa 1:18), and become students, disciples, and followers of Jesus Christ (Matt 28:19-20; 2 Tim 2:2). Instead, becoming like a little child means that we maintain the wonderful and beautiful characteristics and qualities of children that life in this sinful world tends to beat out of us.

Like what?

Like tenderness of conscience. Openness about emotions and feelings. Creativity and imagination.[7] Wonder and awe. Joy. Eternal hope. Playfulness and humor. Trust. Easy forgiveness. Undying love. Boundless exuberance and energy. Always thinking the best about life and other people. Being willing to learn and grow. These are the sort of qualities that tend to define children, but which get stripped out of people as they encounter the sin and brokenness of this world.

As adults, we get bored with flowers, bugs, and sunsets. We lose delight in talking with others about nothing. We become jaded and disinterested. Adults hold grudges, harbor fears, and stay angry. Adults refuse to forgive. Adults remember slights. Adults lose hope because their hopes have been dashed and destroyed so many time. Adults do things "because they've always been done that way" and have trouble imagining anything different.

But children do not behave in any of these ways. Nor did Jesus. One of the things that attracted people to Jesus is that He was "childlike." Does this mean He lacked wisdom and understanding? Far from it. Jesus was "childlike" because He was full of the wonder of life, the hope for humanity, and the beauty of creation.

[7] Cf. Gregory Boyd, *Seeing is Believing* (Grand Rapids: Baker, 2004) and Walter Brueggemann, *The Prophetic Imagination* (Minneapolis: Augsburg Fortress, 2001).

Jesus lived in awe of life, awe of God, and awe of humanity.

And this awe was contagious. People who saw how Jesus lived began to see how life should be lived. Jesus revealed how God intended life to be lived. In other words, those who begin to live life like Jesus are those who begin to see heaven come down to earth. They begin to see the rule and reign of God unfold in their own life with all its beauty, majesty, glory, and creativity. This is what Jesus Himself lived, and this is what Jesus invited others to live also. He taught that if you want to experience God's life in this life (the kingdom of heaven), then you need to become like a little child once again.

So yes, ask questions. Lots of questions. But also have fun. Laugh. Play. Imagine. Sing. Dance. Hope. Dream. Forgive. Create. Trust. Live life to the full. Be excited. Be adventuresome. Be tender of heart. And most of all, love. When you live this way, you will become like a little child, and will see the kingdom of heaven rise again in your life.

FAITH AND "THE FAITH"

The fourth clarification about faith is the difference between "faith" and "the faith." There are various texts in the New Testament which include the definite article "the" before the noun "faith" (called the *articular* use).

Most often in the Greek New Testament, the word "faith" appears without the definite article (called the *anarthrous* use). When the word "faith" does not have the article "the" in front of it, the word can be understood as defined and explained in this book.

However, there are several texts in the New Testament which include the definite article before the noun. Most English Bibles translate this phrase as "the faith" (cf. Acts 6:7; 13:8; 14:22; 16:5; Rom 1:5; 1 Cor 16:13; 2 Cor 13:5; Gal 1:23; 3:23; 6:10; Eph 4:13; Php 1:25-27; Col 1:23; 1 Tim 3:9-4:6; 5:8; 6:10, 21; 2 Tim 2:18; 3:8; 4:7; Titus 1:13; Jude 3). If we try to understand these texts as referring to "a persuasion or conviction that something is true" many of them will not make sense. In a few places, the New Testament even seems to contrast "faith" with "the faith" by sometimes including various good works and acts of obedience with "the faith" (e.g., Acts 6:7; 14:22; Rom 1:5; 1 Cor 16:13; 2 Cor 13:5).

It is better, therefore, to recognize that the articular use of faith in the Greek New Testament does not refer to "faith" or "belief" itself, but to the belief *system* of Christianity. In other words, while "faith" refers to the conviction that a particular statement is true, "the faith" refers to all the beliefs and behaviors which comprise basic Christianity. So "the faith" is a shorthand way for New Testament writers to speak about "the Christian faith." This is similar to how we might talk and write about "the Buddhist faith," or "the Muslim faith." All such terms are shorthand ways of referring to the traditions, beliefs, practices, and behaviors that are included within those individual "religions."[8]

So while "faith" can be defined as a persuasion or conviction that something is true, the articular term "the faith" refers more comprehensively to all the fundamental Christian teachings and practices that separate followers of Jesus from followers of some other teacher or world religion. "'The faith' is the body of truth that has been delivered to us from God."[9] Therefore, "the faith" is a phrase used to describe the comprehensive system of basic Christian creed and conduct. It refers to what Christians teach in regard to both beliefs and behaviors. This understanding helps make sense of most of the New Testament texts which refer to "the faith." A few of these texts will be examined more closely in the following chapter.

FAITH AND FAITHFULNESS

The final clarification about faith that needs to be made is how it differs from the word faithfulness. The reason this is important is because there are numerous authors

---

[8] I don't consider Christianity *a religion*, but there was no better term to describe it in comparison to the various other world religions.

[9] Robert N. Wilkin, *Secure and Sure: Grasping the Promises of God* (Irving, TX: Grace Evangelical Society, 2005), 101.

and teachers today who argue that the biblical concept of "faith" is better understood as "faithfulness," and therefore, it does not primarily refer to what a person knows to be true in their minds, but instead to how a person lives over the course of their life. As a result, these authors argue that the term "faith" in the Bible more rightly refers to loyalty, allegiance, or ongoing obedience.[10] In light of this idea, such authors teach that we receive eternal life from God, not by believing in Jesus for it, but by living a life of faithfulness, allegiance, and obedience to Jesus.

For numerous reasons, it does not seem best to understand the word "faith" (Gk., *pistis*) as "faithfulness." While there does initially seem to be some evidence for this understanding in various biblical and extra-biblical contexts, such a view opens the door for a works-based approach to gaining, proving, or keeping our eternal life, and so should be rejected. After all, if *pistis* can sometimes refer to allegiance, loyalty, or ongoing obedience, then there is nothing to stop someone from saying that most references to faith in the New Testament carry this idea, and therefore, eternal life is not gained by simply believing in Jesus for it, but instead by living loyally and obediently to Him. This is indeed what some argue.[11]

---

[10] See, for example, Michael W. Bates, *Salvation by Allegiance Alone: Rethinking Faith, Works, and the Gospel of Jesus the King* (Grand Rapids: Baker, 2017).

[11] Ibid.

Yet once we properly understand that faith is a conviction or persuasion that something is true, we are then positioned to better understand the various texts in English Bibles which translate *pistis* as faithfulness. When studied in their contexts, we see that these controversial passages do not require for *pistis* to refer to loyalty, allegiance, or ongoing obedience, but could instead refer to a persistent and ongoing faith. Remember, faith is like a light switch. When it comes to the various truths we can believe, faith is either "On" or "Off." If it stays "On" for a long time, then it is persistent faith.

No all beliefs stay "On" all the time. We often change our beliefs due to new evidence that is presented to us. Sometimes we change our beliefs as we learn more about God through Scripture and in fellowship with other believers. In such instances, we turn away from falsehood and embrace the truth, so that our network of beliefs comes to more closely match what is actually true. But we can also stray from the truth and fall into dangerous and unhealthy teachings. It is not uncommon for true believers to fall prey to false teaching so that they come to deny the truth and turn instead toward lies and deceptive ideas. But as long as a Christian maintains a belief in what is actually true, their belief is persistent. This persistent faith is which Scripture invites us to strive and long for. The texts that seem to require a translation of "faithfulness" are not referring to allegiance and obedience, but to this ongoing and persistent faith.[12] It is a faith that remains.

This is even true when the Bible refers to the faith of God or the faith of Jesus. It is not necessary to understand these texts as referring to the faithfulness of God or the faithfulness of Jesus. Since faith is the knowledge, conviction, or persuasion that something is true, then it is obvious that both God and Jesus can have faith. Indeed, the Trinitarian God is the only being in the universe who has perfect faith. All other beings in the universe do not have perfect knowledge of all things, and therefore, do not believe or know all things. Only God's faith is eternally perfect and persistent. Since faith or belief is the conviction that something is true, God knows everything that is true, and therefore, believes it and will always believe it.

Furthermore, He even has faith toward us. He knows what is true about us, even when we do not (Rom 3:3-4). He also knows what *will be* true about us, and He speaks these things to us so that we might be inspired by His testimony toward us to believe these things as well. God wants us to live as He sees us; not as we see ourselves. God believes in us and invites us to believe in Him so that together, our belief will bring God's vision of the future into reality.

---

[12] Besides, when various biblical authors *do* want to refer to loyalty or allegiance, there are perfectly fine Greek words which they can (and do) use to refer to these concepts. We must let faith remain faith and stop trying to add works into it.

This understanding helps clarify some of the tricky texts which seem to require "faithfulness" as a translation of *pistis*. Such texts do not refer to allegiance or ongoing obedience, but to an ongoing and persistent belief. And this belief can lead to other beliefs as well. For example, once we have believed in Jesus for eternal life, this does not mean that faith has no more place in the life of the believer. Just as we have received Jesus Christ, so also we must continue to walk with Him (Col 2:6). And how is it that we received Jesus? By faith. So we are to continue our life with Him by faith as well.

This is not only true because ongoing faith gives us the best life possible with Jesus, but also because other truths we can believe depend on continuing to believe previous truths. Remember that all of our beliefs are interconnected like a vast Excel spreadsheet. Many of the more advanced truths and ideas on this spreadsheet will not be discovered and cannot be believed unless we maintain our belief in some of the earlier, foundational truths. In other words, future faith builds upon our former faith. Believing simple and elementary things allows us to later believe more difficult and hard things. This is what Paul means when it talks about going from "faith to faith" (cf. Rom 1:17) and when he refers to faith as a fruit of the Spirit (Gal 5:22). As we walk with God in faith and by the Spirit, we grow in our faith and come to believe things that draw us closer to God and make us more like Jesus.

So regardless of which stage of faith we are talking about, faith does not involve ongoing obedience. Faith does not begin with simple belief and then end with allegiance and loyalty. There are no works in faith, for faith is the opposite of works. While faith can lead to works, the presence or absence of works do not necessarily indicate anything one way or another about a person's faith. In all cases, faith is simply being persuaded and convinced about what we have been told. When we believe in Jesus for eternal life, we are persuaded that Jesus, as the author and finisher of our faith, loves us, forgives us, and freely grants eternal life to us, not because of anything we have done but simply and only because of God's grace toward us. No commitment to allegiance or ongoing obedience are required. Therefore, the word *pistis* is not ever properly translated as "faithfulness."[13]

CONCLUSION

With these five clarifications about faith, we have now put on our faith glasses and can see life and Scripture more clearly. We can be less fuzzy in our thinking about faith and can see the individual leaves on the trees of various verses. Many of the passages which previously caused confusion and consternation about whether we

[13] I might be fine with "faithfulness" if it was understood to refer to an ongoing or persistent faith. But since few think of "faithfulness" this way, it is best to not translate *pistis* as faithfulness.

have the right faith or enough faith are now easily understood. This is what the next chapter reveals as we turn to consider several key biblical texts about faith.

CHAPTER 5

UNDERSTANDING SCRIPTURES
ON FAITH

Now that we understand what faith is and is not, and have considered several misconceptions and clarifications about faith, we are now in a position to better understand many tricky biblical texts that refer to faith. Some of these texts have created numerous problems in church history and have caused many Christians great amounts of consternation and fear. If this is true of you, then this final chapter will be helpful. When your understanding about faith is cleared up by the ideas found in this book, your fear about faith is also cleared away. You will understand what the Bible teaches about faith and that your faith rests on a firm foundation.

This chapter does not contain a comprehensive examination of all the verses in the Bible that mention faith. Instead, the Scriptures considered below are representative of the types of passages the Bible contains about faith. By using what we have learned about faith in this book and by seeing how this understanding better helps us grasp the meaning of various biblical texts which mention faith, you will be able to comprehend any other passage about faith as well. Let us begin by looking at Abraham, the "Father of Faith."

GENESIS 12 AND 15

And he believed in the LORD, and He ac-
counted it to him for righteousness
(Gen 15:6).

Genesis 12 and 15 reveal truths about faith by presenting the faith of Abraham.[1] And since Abraham is "the Father of Faith" (or maybe "the Father of Our Faith") these two chapters in Genesis are foundational for understanding faith. Since the faith of Abraham is so important in Scripture, it is no surprise that Abraham's faith is mentioned in so many contexts. Stephen praises Abraham's faith in Acts 7:2-8. Paul praises the faith of Abraham in Romans 4 and Galatians 3. The author of Hebrews places great emphasis on the faith of Abraham in Hebrews 11, the "Hall of Faith." And James connects Abraham's faith with Abraham's obedience in James 2:21-24 (a passage that will be considered below). Therefore, since Abraham provides the premier example of faith in the Bible, it is important to understand what he believed and how his faith worked.

---

[1] For the sake of consistency, I will refer to him as "Abraham" even though his name was not changed until Genesis 17:5.

It is important to begin where the faith of Abraham began. Many people believe that Abraham was just minding his own business when God showed up and told him to go to Canaan, so Abraham got up and went. In light of this, we say "What amazing faith! Abraham didn't know much about God, but God told him to go, so he got up and went! He never doubted; he never questioned; he never looked back." But the truth is that this is not what happened at all. Abraham's faith worked just like ours.

To many, the story of Abraham begins in Genesis 12:1 when God comes to him and says "Get up and go." Most think that when Abraham heard God's instructions at age seventy-five, he believed what God said and immediately departed Haran for Canaan (Gen 12:4). But some careful study of the text reveals something else entirely. There are seven key insights about Abraham's faith we can learn from these chapters.

First of all, Genesis 12 does not make any mention of Abraham's faith. The faith of Abraham is not mentioned until Genesis 15:6. So although Abraham does depart Haran and travel to Canaan in Genesis 12:4, there is nothing from the text that indicates Abraham did this because he believed what God said. We don't know what he believed.

Second, the call of God in Genesis 12 to get up and go is not the first time God had said this to Abraham. In fact, God initially called Abraham many years before, when he was living in Ur. According to Joshua 24:2, Abraham was an idol-worshiper when he lived in Ur, and Stephen says in Acts 7:2-4 that it was when Abraham lived in Ur that God first told him to leave his country and relatives and go to a new land. And though it appears that Abraham did get up and go, he did not leave his family. Instead, he took his father, Terah, and his nephew, Lot, with him. Furthermore, he didn't go to Canaan. Instead, he only traveled to Haran, which was northwest of Ur.

We do not know how long Abraham lived in Haran before God told him *again* to follow God where He would lead. But the evidence seems to indicate that once again, Abraham did not believe and obey. Though God told Abraham to leave his father and his relatives, Abraham waited in Haran until his father died (Gen 11:31-32; Acts 7:4). I do not think it true obedience to "leave your father" if you wait until your father leaves you by dying. Regardless, when Abraham is seventy-five years old, he finally sets out to see where God is leading him.

Third, when Abraham finally arrives in Canaan, the land where God was leading him, one of the first things he does is leave for Egypt (Gen 12:10-20). He does not seem to believe that God will be able to provide for him in this land, even though God led him here. For all we know, the famine in Canaan which caused Abraham to leave for Egypt might actually have been the means by which Abraham could have gained large sections of Canaan for himself and his family. But since Abraham fled to Egypt, the only land which God ever "gave" to Abraham was a small burial plot which Abraham purchased at great expense as a burial plot for Sarah (Gen 23:15-16).[2]

Fourth, even when Abraham's faith is finally mentioned in Genesis 15:6, Abraham still asks for evidence from God so that he can believe what God has said. Abraham doesn't place blind faith in God, but wants proof. He basically says, "How shall I know that what you are saying is true?" (Gen 15:8). This is not wrong, since faith often depends on evidence, but it is certainly not the blind faith that many attribute to Abraham. Beyond this, Abraham is now around 85 years old (Gen 16:16) and had been journeying with God for over ten years. He had seen how God provided for him and protected him, and yet even now, when he finally believes what God says, he asks for evidence to support and confirm his belief.

Fifth, and maybe most significantly, Abraham's faith did not keep him from frequent doubt and sin. For example, even though his father, Tereh, had sired Abraham when Terah was 130, Abraham wondered if God could let him have a child when he was 100.[3] And when

---

[2] I am not saying, nor does the text, that God sent the famine.

[3] See this article for an explanation of the numbers and what Abraham was possibly thinking: https://www.apologeticspress.org/apcontent.aspx?category=6&article=665. Last Accessed Mach 31, 2018.

it comes to sin, many of the moral failures Abraham committed before he believed are identical to the moral failures he committed after he believed. Abraham lied about his wife and put her in danger both before and after he believed (Gen 12:10-20; 20:1-18). Further-more, it is only *after* Abraham believed that he slept with his wife's maidservant, Hagar. People who say that "true and genuine faith leads to a changed life and a perseverance in good works" cannot point to Abraham, the father of faith, as an example. Abraham's faith did not necessarily lead to better actions and morality.

Of course, there is one action that is said to reveal Abraham's faith most clearly, and it is the action he is most known for: the near-sacrifice of Isaac on the altar in Genesis 22. This is the sixth truth we learn about Abraham's faith. We are not exactly sure how old Abra-ham was when he set out for Mount Moriah, but since Isaac was "a lad" (Gen 22:5) this likely means that Isaac was at least ten years old,[4] making Abraham at least 110 (Gen 21:5). So this great act of faith came 25 years after Abraham initially believed in God and was justified, and at least 35 years after Abraham initially started following God. This is not what we call an immediate, life-changing transformation where a person who was an idol-worshiper one day is a committed and devoted fol-lower of God the next. No, this was a 35-year journey

---

[4] He could not have been older than 36 (Gen 17:17; 21:5; 23:1).

with God, full of false starts, doubts, questions, fears, and moral failures. Just like our life.

The father of faith in the Bible reveals that faith is not monumental, all-inclusive, once-for-all conviction to follow and obey God no matter what. To the contrary, faith is about taking one little step at a time with God, and often in a way that includes backward steps as well. Faith requires time to build and grow. Faith requires evidence and experience. Faith allows for the setbacks of sin and moral failure. This is just like our faith as well. Abraham is the father of faith, not because he had such amazing faith, but because he shows us what faith looks like and how faith works.[5]

Seventh, note something else about Abraham's faith. We are told in Genesis 15 that Abraham believed God and God credited him with righteousness (Gen 15:6). But Abraham doesn't look or act much like a righteous believer for the next several chapters. Therefore, some argue that the "proof" or "evidence" of Abraham's justification is found in Genesis 22 where he nearly sacrifices his son, Isaac, on an altar. Those who hold this view often use James 2:21-24 as support.

James 2 will be discussed in more detail later in this chapter, but note for now that no action of Abraham in Genesis 22 gives proof or evidence that he was in fact declared righteous by God, or that he had believed in

---

[5] We can also say that Abraham is the father of faith in that he is the father of "the faith." In other words, he is the founder of the Jewish faith.

God 25 years earlier. To the contrary, Hebrews 11:17-19 reveals that when Abraham offered his son Isaac on the altar, he did this because he believed that God could raise Isaac from the dead. This is a completely different belief than the belief of Abraham in Genesis 15.

In Genesis 15, Abraham believed that God would give him descendants that outnumber the stars, whereas in Genesis 22, Abraham believed that God could raise Isaac from the dead. On the Excel spreadsheet of belief, these are two completely different cells. Certainly, the second is connected to, or depends upon, the first. Abraham knew that before he could have a multitude of descendants, he first had to have one descendant. And while he initially tried to obtain this first descendant through Hagar, this was not part of God's initial plan, and so Abraham eventually had Isaac as well.

So when Abraham was told to sacrifice Isaac, Abraham's new belief—that God would raise Isaac from the dead—was based upon his previous belief, that God would give Abraham many descendants. The two beliefs are connected, but they are not the same beliefs. This reveals that even with Abraham, there was an interconnected network of beliefs that changed and grew as Abraham matured in his relationship with God.

But since this is true, what exactly did Abraham believe in Genesis 15? People sometimes wonder how Abraham could have been justified by God when it appears that all he believed was that he would have descendants that outnumbered the stars. According to the New Testament, however, people are justified, or receive eternal life, when they believe in Jesus for it. Abraham clearly could not have believed in Jesus (for the birth of Jesus was still 2000 years in the future), but it also does not appear that Abraham believed that a future Messiah was coming. In other words, there is no indication in the text that Abraham believed what God said *about a Messiah who would give eternal life.* Instead, Abraham believed what God said, namely, that he would have many descendants. How is this justifying faith? Can someone be justified by believing any random truth from God, whether or not it has anything to do with righteousness received through faith in Jesus?

The answer to this question is that Abraham knew more than we think and more than the Bible records. We know this because Jesus Himself says that "Abraham rejoiced to see My day; he saw it and was glad" (John 8:56). What did Jesus mean by this? We don't really know, and neither did the Jews in His day (John 8:57). Some speculate that when the text says that the LORD appeared to Abraham (Gen 12:7), it was actually Jesus who appeared to him. Others posit that Melchizedek was actually a pre-incarnate Jesus (cf. Gen 14:18-24; Heb 7:1-4). Others think that one of the three men who visited Abraham might have been Jesus (Gen 18:1-33). The truth, however, is we don't really know what Jesus meant when He said that Abraham had seen His day. It does reveal to us, however, that Abraham knew more than the biblical text records, and that somehow, Abraham truly did know Jesus.

I also believe that Abraham would have been familiar with the story of Adam and Eve, especially since the original Eden was likely in the same region as Ur. Therefore, Abraham would have known about the promised seed of the woman who would crush the head of the serpent and restore humanity to our rightful place within this world (Gen 3:15). It is quite possible that Abraham saw his calling by God as the next step in the fulfilment of this prophecy. Therefore, whatever Abraham believed about a coming Messiah, or however it was that he saw the day of Jesus, it is quite likely that Abraham believed that God was somehow going to fix the problems of this world through the child that would come from him and Sarah. He might not have known exactly how, but he believed what God said, and as a result, God credited him with righteousness.

Since Abraham is the father of faith, with all of his struggles, failures, doubts, and yes, successes, it is no surprise to see a similar blending of faith and doubt, success and failure, all the way throughout the stories of Scripture. So when you see similar struggles in your own life, this does not mean that your faith is weak or that you have false faith. Quite to the contrary, it means that your faith is perfectly normal, and that God is patiently walking by your side, just as He did with Abraham, calling you to take one more step with Him. Don't give up on Him, because He has not given up on you. Believe in Him and what He says, because He believes in you.

These same themes of faith are found throughout the rest of the Hebrew Scriptures, and so rather than look at several other similar examples, let us turn instead to the New Testament to see what we can learn about faith from the teachings of Jesus and the writings of the apostles.

MATTHEW 6:30

Now if God so clothes the grass of the field, which today is, and tomorrow is thrown into the oven, will He not much more clothe you, O you of little faith?

Matthew 6:30 causes some people to fear that they do not have enough faith or the right kind of faith in order to please God. The reason for this fear is that Jesus talks about those who have "little faith." The theme of "great faith" versus "little faith" is compared and contrasted throughout the Gospel of Matthew (8:10 vs. 8:26; 9:22-24; 14:31 vs. 15:28; 16:8; 17:20; 21:21) and so it is important to understand what is meant by this term "little faith."[6]

---

[6] For an excellent explanation of the difference between great faith and little faith, see Bob Wilkin, "Should We Rethink the Idea of Degrees of Faith?" *JOTGES* (Fall, 20016), https://faithalone.org/

The concepts of little faith and great faith were discussed in a previous chapter, but a short summary will be helpful here.

Little faith and great faith is not about having more or less faith, or a higher percentage or degree of faith. Faith does not work like that. We can either believe something or not believe it. When it comes to an individual statement or proposition, we either believe it or not. In our Excel spreadsheet of beliefs, the cell is either "On" or "Off." Yet some of the statements in these cells are easy to believe, while others are more difficult. The propositions of quantum physics are much harder to understand and believe than the basic mathematical fact that 2+2=4.

This applies to theology as well. On the scale of difficult theological truths, it is easier to believe that "I exist" than it is to believe that "God exists." It is easier to believe that "A man named Jesus existed" than it is to believe that "This Jesus is God." As you can see, each theological proposition has a relative level of difficulty. It is this relative level of difficulty that Jesus is referring to when He talks about little faith and great faith. Those who have little faith do not believe some of the relatively simple truths, whereas those who have great faith believe things that are more difficult to believe and which almost nobody believes. This is what we see from Matthew 6:30.

journal/2006ii/01%20Wilkin%20-%20great%20faith.pdf Last Accessed April 2, 2008.

To begin with, it is important to note that Jesus is not teaching about how to receive eternal life, or any related concept. He is teaching about God's protection and provision for His disciples. As evidence of this provision, Jesus points to God's tender care for sparrows and flowers (Matt 6:25-30). Since God feeds the birds and clothes the lilies, will not also God feed and clothe the disciples? In other words, the evidence is all around the disciples that God will feed and clothe them. They are not asked to believe such a thing in spite of the evidence, but in light of it. Yet the disciples do not believe this, and so Jesus chides them for having "little faith." Instead of believing, they worry about tomorrow and wonder if God will provide.

If we are honest, nearly all of us have "little faith" in this regard. After all, we have plenty of evidence to support our lack of faith. If we really look at the birds of the air and lilies of the field as Jesus instructs, the picture is not as rosy as He presents it. Millions of birds suffer and die each and every day around the world. They are killed by cats, slaughtered for food, broken by storms, hit by cars, fly into closed windows, and drop dead from disease. It's worse with plants. Innumerable plants and flowers die every day from fire, harvest, disease, drought, and human carelessness.

So while there truly is much evidence that God cares for these parts of His creation, this does not mean that all birds and plants live happy, healthy, carefree, and pain-free lives. God's creation is "red in tooth and claw"[7] and often gets damaged through famine and fire. Therefore, it is understandable that we humans often doubt God's ability or desire to care for us. Indeed, when we look at billions of people starving all over the world, and millions of people dying from war and famine, the evidence against Jesus' words seems to be stronger than the evidence in favor.

I was once conducting a Bible study with some non-Christian friends when we came to this passage. I had previously told them that they did not need to believe what they were reading, but should only consider what the Bible was saying, and react honestly to it. Several of the people in this group had experienced great pain and difficulties in life, and had abandoned or rejected God as a result. So when they read these words of Jesus, one of them said, "This is bull$#!t. Look at all the people dying overseas. Look at the girls being sold into sex slavery. Look at the people starving in Africa or even here in our own country. If I had been there listening to Jesus when He said this, I would have called Him out on it."

My friend had a good point and I told him so. Most Christians are too afraid to honestly say what they think about some of what they read in the Bible (or even to think honestly about the Bible). This is why it is so refreshing to study the Bible with non-Christians. If you ever get the chance to attend a Bible study with atheists,

[7] See the poem "In Memoriam" by Alfred, Lord Tennyson.

I highly recommend it. They feel the freedom to speak their mind and object to what they read. By allowing their unbiased eyes to see what our biased eyes cannot, you gain great insight into some of the difficult texts of Scripture.

I wish an atheist had been around when Jesus spoke the words of Matthew 6:30. I wish someone listening to Jesus had objected to what He said. Of all the questions the disciples asked Jesus, why didn't one of them ask Jesus for some clarification about this statement? The idea that God will care for us as He cares for birds and plants is just not very reassuring. Jesus says we have "little faith" if we don't believe God will provide for us, and yet the evidence Jesus presents seems to pretty clearly show that God will not always protect and provide for us. Why didn't the disciples push back? Why didn't Peter raise his hand and say, "Eh … Jesus … you may want to rethink your analogy. Remember what we saw on our way here this morning? There was that nest of dead baby birds on the ground. Did God take care of them? Then there was that donkey eating all those flowers. What about them?"

But nobody asked, and so no clarification was offered.

Yet there was a later follower of Jesus who does seem to have asked this question. Better yet, he seems to have an answer to this question as well, and he wrote about it in Scripture. But before we look at who this was and what he learned, let us first see what we can learn from Jesus.

We must begin by recognizing that since Jesus so clearly *seems* to be wrong about God's care and provision, this can only mean that *we* are wrong in how we have understood Him. Jesus is never wrong; but we often are wrong in how we understand His words. So we must assume that in this instance, we have misunderstood what Jesus is teaching about the protection and provision of God. Let us consider three insights from the text that will help us better understand the words of Jesus.

First, much of the Sermon on the Mount falls into the biblical genre of "Wisdom Literature." Wisdom Literature never provides universal rules for how life *always* works. It instead presents general principles and themes that help us navigate through life. Much like the book of Proverbs, this sermon by Jesus provides broad overarching principles about how life works in the kingdom of God. So the teaching about God's provision and protection is a general principle, not a universal rule.

Second, note that this protection and provision is only in reference to food and clothing. It is not about long life, health, or freedom from pain or sickness. It is about daily sustenance only. So even though Jesus is only providing a general guideline, it doesn't apply to all of life or to all aspects of life, but only to God's daily provision for food and clothing.

The third thing to note is that Jesus provides this teaching within the context of seeking the kingdom of God (Matt 6:33). It appears that these promises are primarily directed toward those who seek first the kingdom. In other words, the promised provision and protection of God is not a blanket promise for all people everywhere. It is instead a promise for disciples of Jesus who seek to spread the kingdom of God through their life and actions. Since Jesus teaches this truth about God's provision within the context of His "Discipleship Manual" (Matt 5–7), it is no surprise that the promises He makes for provision apply primarily to those who are His disciples and who are carrying out the work of the kingdom.

This third insight is specifically applied by Jesus to His disciples when He later instructs them to carry the message of the kingdom of God into the surrounding countryside (Luke 9:1-6; 10:1-12). He says that as they carry out the work of the kingdom, they should not take food, money, or extra clothing with them, but should expect that their daily needs of food and shelter would be met by the people to whom they ministered.

This brings us back around to the person in Scripture who might have wondered how this promise of God's provision really worked and what he said about it. Who was this person? It was James, the brother of Jesus. James didn't always follow Jesus, but after Jesus died and rose again, James became one of the leaders in the early church (Acts 15:13, 19; Gal 2:9). And many sections of the letter that bears his name serve as a commentary on how to apply various portions of the Sermon on the Mount.

So when James writes that "If a brother or sister is naked and destitute of daily food …" (Jas 2:15), we are to immediately remember what Jesus said in Matthew 6 about God providing clothing and daily food to His followers. James has noted that some people in God's church truly do go without clothing and daily food. Doesn't this contradict what Jesus taught, that God will provide food and clothing for His people? In James 2:15-16, James solves this dilemma by basically saying, "If you see someone who doesn't have clothing and food, don't quote Matthew 6:30 at them, saying that God will provide for their needs. And don't pray for them either. What good is that? Prayer and Bible verses will not put clothing on their back or food in their belly. Instead, give them something to wear and something to eat."

So when Jesus says, "God will provide for your daily needs," James clarifies by saying, "Yes, and how does God do this? Through one another as we take care of each other." Therefore, when someone's needs are *not* being met, it is not that God has failed, but that the church has failed to obey God. When people are starving and homeless and we cry out to God, "Why don't you do something?" God cries out to us, "Why don't *you* do something?"

This clarification by James helps us understand the words of Jesus in Matthew 6:30. Those who seek the kingdom of God will never be in want for daily food and clothing because we will always be providing food and clothing for others who need it, and they will be providing it for us.

So Jesus was right all along. He was primarily teaching a truth to His disciples about how their needs for food and clothing would be met as they followed His instructions to carry the message of the gospel to the surrounding region. These needs would be met through the provision of the people to whom they ministered. The disciples should have known that God would provide for them in exactly this way, for as they lived and walked with Jesus, they had seen time and time again that all of their needs for food and clothing had been met by other human beings who gave it to them.

This is why Jesus chides His disciples for having "little faith." The Greek word Jesus uses for "little faith" is *oligōpistos.* This word is not found anywhere else outside of Scripture, and within Scripture, only Jesus uses this term. Some postulate that Jesus coined this phrase.[8] It is also important to recognize that Jesus only uses this word in reference to the faith of His disciples. He never chides anyone else other than His disciples for having

---

[8] Wilkin, "Should We Rethink the Idea of Degrees of Faith?", 8.

"little faith." Apparently, since the disciples were following Jesus around, listening to His teachings, and observing His miracles, there were many instances where they should have known better than the average person and more readily believed some of what He taught. Because of their proximity to Jesus, more was expected of them than He would expect of others.

If you don't believe what Jesus says here, it is not necessarily because you have little faith. Instead, it is because you have not yet had the benefit that the disciples had. You have not yet walked with Jesus long enough to see Him miraculously provide time and time again. The disciples had seen this, but they still did not believe. However, if you are seeking first the kingdom of God, and as you have gone about God's work in this way, have seen Jesus provide for you time and time again, but you are still not sure He will provide for your basic needs of today, then yes, you might qualify for having "little faith."

But if you are a non-Christian or a new Christian, or if you are living for yourself rather than for the kingdom of God, or if you have not seen God provide food and clothing for you time and time again just when you need it, then you have no reason to believe that God will meet your basic needs today. You have little evidence to support this promise and little experience in seeing that it is true. If this is your situation, then even if you do not believe what Jesus says, you do not have "little faith." Why not? Because without any evidence or experience, the truth that God will provide for your daily food and clothing is quite difficult to believe.

The disciples, on the other hand, were expected to believe this because of what they had seen, heard, and experienced with Jesus. This is why Jesus gently chides them for not believing it. After everything they had seen and done with Jesus, it should have been a simple thing for them to believe that God would provide for their basic needs of food and clothing as they went about their work of expanding the kingdom of God. But they did not believe this, and so Jesus said they had "little faith." They did not believe something that should have been obvious and easy for them to believe, even though it is not obvious and easy for all of us.

Jesus' other references to "little faith" in the Gospels can be understood in a similar way (Matt 8:26; 14:31; 16:8; Luke 12:28). This term does not mean that the disciples of Jesus needed a higher degree or greater percentage of faith. Again, faith does not work like that. There are no degrees of faith. Rather, it means is that the disciples did not believe something that they should have easily believed. Though they did believe many truths, there are some truths they did not believe which Jesus expected them to easily believe, based on the evidence provided to them through His life, ministry, teachings, and example. Since they didn't believe these truths, He chided them for having "little faith."

If you have trouble believing some of the things Jesus chided His disciples for not believing, do not beat yourself up. It is unlikely that He is chiding you for having "little faith." Why not? Because we do not have many of the same benefits and blessings that the disciples had through their close proximity to Jesus. We do not have the evidence and experience that they had. Therefore, some of the things that He expected them to easily believe, might be very difficult for us to believe. But we might come to believe some of these things as He walks with us and teaches us new truths each and every day.

In fact, if you do come to believe some of the truths which should have been simple for the disciples to believe, Jesus might actually praise you for having great faith. The simplicity or difficulty of believing a particular truth depends entirely on how much evidence and experience a person has. Those with "little faith" do not believe truths that they should believe in light of how much they know and have seen. On the other hand, those with "great faith" are those who do believe truths that most people would not believe with the same level of knowledge and experience. This is what we see from Matthew 8:10 where Jesus praises a man for having great faith.

MATTHEW 8:10 (MATT 15:28; LUKE 7:9)

*When Jesus heard it, He marveled, and
said to those who followed, "Assuredly, I
say to you, I have not found such great
faith, not even in Israel!"*

There are two kinds of faith that amazed Jesus: great
faith and little faith. As seen above, there were times
when Jesus marveled at the little faith of His disciples
(cf. Matt 6:30; 8:26; 14:31; 16:8; Luke 4:14-30; 12:28).
But in Matthew 8:10, Jesus was impressed by the great
faith of a Gentile. The Gentile was a Roman Centurion
who had a sick servant at home, and he requested that
Jesus heal his servant. After a brief conversation, Jesus
said, "I have not found such great faith, not even in Israel!"[9] Why did Jesus say this man had great faith?

Since we have properly understood that "little faith"
occurs when a person does not believe easy truths, or
truths that they clearly should believe based on the
knowledge and evidence presented to them, then this
means that "great faith" is the exact opposite. Great
faith believes difficult truths, or truths for which there is
little evidence. Those with great faith believe truths that
few other people believe. "Great faith is not some higher
level of conviction. It is believing something that is
harder to believe, something that is contrary to what

[9] You can read my sermon on Luke 7:1-10 by visiting
https://redeeminggod.com/sermons/luke/luke_7_1-10/. Last Accessed December 19, 2018.

most people believe."[10] So "great faith" and "little faith" have nothing to do with the size, amount, or degree of a person's faith. Instead, these terms describe the relative level of difficulty of the truths that are believed.

So in Matthew 8:10, Jesus praises a Roman Centurion for having great faith. What did the Centurion believe that few others believe? He believed two advanced truths that are quite rare for people to believe (even today). First, he believed in his own lack of merit. Though he was courteous, humble, and a good man, though he loved the Jewish people and built a synagogue for them, he knew he didn't deserve anything from God, or from Jesus Christ. Despite his high standing and all he had done, he knew he was unworthy to meet with Jesus (Matt 8:8). Most people do not believe this. Most people think they do deserve favors from God. Most people think they are pretty good people and that God owes them something. It is much harder to believe that all we have and all we are given is simply and only by the grace of God. But the centurion believed this, and told Jesus that he was not worthy to have Jesus visit his house.

The second thing the Centurion believed was that healing could be done at a distance. He believed in the divine authority of Jesus, even over sickness and disease through space and time. He likened Jesus to a military commander who simply had to give orders for them to be followed (Matt 8:9). He knew that whatever Jesus

[10] Wilkin, "Should We Rethink the Idea of Degrees of Faith?", 10.

commanded would be done, even if Jesus was not present where the healing was to take place. He knew that the words of Jesus were sufficient to accomplish whatever He said.

Most people do not believe this. Even today, most people believe that if a person is going to be healed, they need to be touched by the person praying for them. They believe that they have to go visit the healer, and have the healer lay hands on them, say special prayers over them, and anoint them with oil. If a person was seeking healing for their friend and they want to one of the "miracle healers" of today for help, and the healer said, "Go home, your friend will be fine," that person would feel like they had been ignored, slighted, or brushed off.

But this Centurion knew differently. The Centurion believed some truths that few others believed. He believed that if Jesus wanted to heal someone, He could do it with a simple word and from a great distance. He told Jesus, "Only speak a word, and my servant will be healed" (Matt 8:8). This truly is great faith, and few believe such an idea, either in the days of Jesus or today. As a result, Jesus marveled at this man's great faith, and healed his servant from a distance, simply by the power of His word.

All of the other "great faith" passages in the Bible can be understood in similar ways. The context always reveals that someone is believing something that is difficult to believe, and which few other people believe. So great faith is not a large amount of faith or a high percentage of faith. Great faith simply believes truths that are difficult to believe.

Before we move on, note that "great faith" for one person might not be "great faith" for someone else. The faith of this Centurion was "great faith" because he had very little experience with Jesus. He likely had not seen many of Jesus' miracles or heard any of his teachings. Yet the disciples had. So if the disciples had actually believed what this Centurion believed, it likely would not have been considered "great faith" for them. It is simply what they should have believed, based on the evidence that had been presented to them up to this point. Since the Centurion had very little of this evidence, and yet arrived at this belief based on what he knew from the Roman military, he was praised for having "great faith."

When people arrive at advanced truths and difficult concepts early in their relationship with God, they can be praised for having great faith. But people who have more knowledge, experience, and understanding of the things of God and how God works are expected to understand and believe some of these more advanced truths. If they still do not believe, based on everything they have seen and heard, then their lack of faith could even be called "little faith."

Nevertheless, regardless of whether a person has great faith or little faith, Jesus is still adamant that even the smallest faith can accomplish great things. This is what He teaches with the image of the mustard seed in Matthew 17:20.

MATTHEW 17:20 (LUKE 17:6)

So Jesus said to them, "Because of your unbelief; for assuredly, I say to you, if you have faith as a mustard seed, you will say to this mountain, 'Move from here to there,' and it will move; and nothing is impossible for you."

The disciples wanted to know why they were unable to cast out a particular demon. Initially, Jesus says it was because of their unbelief, and He goes on to talk about faith like a mustard seed. He says that even faith as small as a mustard seed can move mountains with a simple word. But since nobody has ever moved a mountain by simply telling it to move, many get confused by this teaching of Jesus. What did He mean and how can this teaching be applied?

It seems that there are numerous layers of meaning to these words of Jesus. First, it seems obvious that Jesus was not primarily referring to literal mountains (but see below). Instead, Jesus was symbolically referring to "mountain-sized" obstacles, such as this stubborn demon that would not be cast out. In this case, Jesus isn't *literally* saying that a person could move a mountain by having the proper "mountain-moving" faith. Instead, He is teaching that when we encounter insurmountable problems in our life, we must believe that God can handle them.

Second, this passage must be read in light of Matthew 13:31-32, where Jesus says that although a mustard seed is the smallest of all the seeds, it grows into a large tree so that even birds can nest it its branches. When read in connection with this text, Jesus is reminding His disciples that big things come from small beginnings. The Kingdom of God will eventually cover the entire earth, but it begins and is spread with small, seemingly insignificant ideas and actions.

Indeed, in the context, Jesus goes on to say that this kind of demon "does not go out except by prayer and fasting" (Matt 17:21). What does fasting and prayer have to do with faith that can cast out stubborn demons? It doesn't seem like one would lead to the other. What does fasting have to do with demons? Jesus is saying that as a person roots themselves in small, seemingly insignificant, Kingdom-focused actions such as prayer and fasting, their faith and relationship with God will grow, and they will eventually have the faith to cast out a demon with a word, just as Jesus does (Matt 17:18). Through prayer and fasting, people come to understand and believe new and deeper truths about God and how the spiritual realm works. In this way, small activities like prayer and fasting can lead to the type of faith that is able to cast out demons.

This understanding is aided by the third layer of meaning from this verse. Like many of Jesus' teachings, He was likely using an actual object that was in view of the disciples to serve as the illustration for His teaching. When He spoke of the birds of the air and the lilies of the field in Matthew 6:30, it is likely because there were some of these nearby. Similarly, when Jesus speaks here of a mountain, it seems likely that there was a mountain nearby to which He directed the gaze of His disciples. So to which mountain might Jesus have pointed?

One of my seminary professors believed that Jesus was referring to Herodium, which is a mountain that Herod literally moved from one place to another so that he could build a palace for himself. The place was originally a small hill, but Herod wanted to make it the largest mountain in the region so that he could build his palace on the peak. So he directed his laborers to move a second, nearby mountain and place it on top of the first. If this is the mountain Jesus referred to, then He was saying, "Just as Herod had a vision for the future, and moved an entire mountain, one shovelful at a time, to achieve that vision, so also, if you believe what I have taught about the future Kingdom of God, then it can be inaugurated one prayer and one fast at a time."

This *application* of Jesus' meaning is likely correct, but it seems doubtful that Jesus could have directed the gaze of His disciples to Herodium, for when Jesus spoke this truth about mustard seed faith, He and His disciples were far north in Caesarea Philippi (17:22, 24) while Herodium was south of Jerusalem, a few miles from Bethlehem. So if a literal mountain is needed to help understand the words of Jesus, it seems that one in the region of Caesarea Philippi is needed.

Some speculate, therefore, that since Jesus and His disciples were likely staying in the area near the foot of Mount Hermon which contained the "Gate of Hades" (cf. Matt 16:18), a deep cave at the foot of the mountain from which the Jordan River flowed. [11] This area of Israel was dedicated to the worship of the god Pan and it was here that many people participated in great parties of feasting and promiscuity. So it is interesting that in the context, Jesus mentions that certain demons can only be cast out with fasting and prayer, which is the exact opposite of what usually happened in this area.

If this is where Jesus and His disciples were located when He spoke these words, it is possible that Jesus motioned toward a nearby hill which we now call "Tel Dan," or "the hill of Dan." Though the significance of

[11]   http://www.bible.ca/archeology/bible-archeology-tel-dan-laish-leshem-micah-Jonathan-jeroboams-king-of-israel-high-place-altar-temple-1340-723bc.htm   http://www.land-of-the-bible.com/Caesarea_Philippi   https://www.teldanexcavations.com/past---present-excavations   http://www.land-of-the-bible.com/Mount_Hermon   http://www.land-of-the-bible.com/The_Ancient_City_of_Dan Last Accessed April 8, 2018.

this hill may have been lost on the disciples of Jesus, it has not been lost on modern Christians. Tel Dan has become one of the most important excavation sites in Israel. It is on this site that archaeologists have discovered the David Inscription, the Gate of Abraham, and the shrine of Jeroboam.

If this is the hill to which Jesus pointed, then His statement about moving the mountain could be seen as prophetic. He would be saying, "If you believe and start digging away at this mountain, it will be moved and you will discover great pieces of biblical history." But this view also seems unlikely. Jesus does not appear to speaking prophetically, and His words would not have been understood this way by His immediate audience, the disciples.

Therefore, it seems that a third mountain might be the best choice. In the immediate context, Jesus has just come down from a high mountain upon which He had been transfigured (17:9). But nobody knows for sure where this mountain is located. It has traditionally been identified as Mount Tabor, southwest of the Sea of Galilee.

But since there was a Roman garrison on the top of Mount Tabor at this time, and since it appears that Jesus and His disciples were about 70 miles north in the region of Caesarea Philippi (16:13), some suggest that the Mount of Transfiguration was actually Mount Hermon, which is the highest mountain in the entire region. It is, of course, conceivable that they traveled from Caesarea Philippi down to Mount Tabor since at least six days passed between the confession of Peter at Caesarea Philippi (Matt 16:13-20) and the Mount of Transfiguration (Matt 17:1-13). There could be additional time between Matthew 16:20 and 16:21.

But if Jesus had been motioning to the Mount of Transfiguration (wherever it was), then what is the significance of directing the gaze of the disciples to this mountain and saying that it could move if they only had faith like a mustard seed? In this case, the move would be symbolic. Jesus had just been transfigured (17:9), and then came to a multitude of people (17:14). These actions are reminiscent of the similar steps of Moses on Mount Sinai when he went up to the mountain to receive the Law, and then came down the mountain with a radiant face to meet the multitudes of people below (Exod 34:29-35).

In this way, Jesus could be saying that the center of faith had now *moved* from the Law of Moses given on Mount Sinai, to the person of Jesus revealed on the Mount of Transfiguration. Jesus is saying, "If you can believe it, the Mountain of God has moved and so has the center of our faith. The Kingdom of God, which grows from a mustard seed, will come through Me; not through the Law of Moses."

Due to the overall significance and message of the ministry and teaching of Jesus, this third option is pre-

ferred. But regardless of *which* mountain Jesus was referring to (*if* there even was an actual mountain to which
He pointed), the message of Jesus about mustard-seed
faith is still clear. The imagery was not intended to teach
that faith comes in tiny amounts. Jesus used this image
of the mustard seed to show that even simple, easy beliefs can lead a person to gain great beliefs if we follow
through to where they lead (Matt 13:31; 17:20; Mark
4:31; Luke 13:19; 17:6).

In other words, just as a small mustard seed can develop into a large plant, so also, small faith can grow
into great faith. A small mustard seed can grow into a
large tree, we can move a mountain one shovel-full at a
time, and even the center of our faith can shift and
change as we allow God to lead and guide us. In all cases, we simply need to believe.

So if you think your faith is small, you do not have
to "muster" up more. It's not about how much faith you
have, but about Who your faith is in and what your
faith believes. When your faith is in God and you follow
Him wherever He leads, you will be led on the greatest
adventure ever imagined to accomplish the greatest
deeds ever done. But all these adventures are traveled
one step at a time, just as mountains are moved one
shovel-full at a time and entire belief systems are transformed one idea at a time. So do you want to move a
mountain? Follow your faith wherever it leads. When
you encounter a mountain in your life, mustard seed

faith looks at it and says, "With God's help, I can move that." Then it gets to work to see it done.

LUKE 12:42-48 (MATT 24:45-51)

And the Lord said, "Who then is the faithful and wise steward, whom his master will make ruler over his household, to give them their portion of food in due season? ... the master of that servant will come on a day when he is not looking for him, and at an hour when he is not aware, and will cut him in two and appoint him his portion with the unbelievers (Luke 12:42, 48).

Luke 12:42-48 (and the parallel passage in Matthew 24:45-51) has caused many to think that true faith will always lead to good works, so that if a person does not have the good works, this proves they were never a believer in the first place and will therefore be sent to hell for eternal punishment. But several details of the text reveal a completely different understanding.

First, the people in the story are all stewards, or servants, of the master. These terms indicate that the people in view are all Christian disciples of Jesus. Second, the fact that they are Christians is supported by the truth that all the servants are looking for the return of their master (initially, at least), which is the return of Jesus. Only Christians look for the return of Jesus.

Third, it is important to note that the adjective used to describe the servants in Luke 12:42 is exactly the same adjective used in Luke 12:48, except that the second is negated. Many translations have the first as "faithful" and the second as "unbelieving." This leads people to conclude that since some servants stopped thinking that the master was going to return and started mistreating their fellow servants, this means that they didn't really believe in the first place. But if our Bible translations were consistent, they should have translated both adjectives as either faithful/unfaithful or as believing/unbelieving.

If the words were translated as faithful/unfaithful, then this teaching of Jesus would not be about whether or not a person truly believed as evidenced by their works, but whether or not a person remained faithful and obedient to Jesus while awaiting His return. In this case, the text is not about who has eternal life and who does not, but rather about who serves Jesus faithfully during their lives while He is away. The blessings received at His return is not eternal life, but eternal reward.

If, however, the words are translated as believing/unbelieving (which is the translation I prefer), the text is still not about who has eternal life and who does not, for the issue that separates the two types of servants is that some believe that the master will return soon while others do not. While all of them initially believe that the master will return soon, some stop believing this. This idea fits with the suggestion proposed previously that where the Bible contains the concept of faithfulness, it is best to understand it as "believing and continuing to believe" a particular truth (or set of truths). This is how the words are used in context here.

Furthermore, the belief or unbelief of the servants is not what guides their behavior. Instead, the servants are guided by whether they are wise or foolish. Servants who are wise perform in ways that the master desires, whereas the foolish servants do not.

But what of the consequences at the end of this teaching by Jesus? Does not the imagery of being cut in two and being beaten with many stripes indicate that Jesus does indeed have hell in view? No. From a realistic, practical perspective, it would be physically impossible for a master to cut his servants in half, and then send them to dwell with other unfaithful servants, where they would then all be beaten with many lashes. Cutting someone in half precludes any further disciplinary action. Therefore, it is clearly hyperbole for the sake of making a point.

The picture of cutting them in two is similar to the idea of being "cut to the heart" (Acts 2:37) or the idea found in Hebrews 4:12 where we learn that the Word of God penetrates to divide soul and spirit, joints and marrow, judging the thoughts and attitudes of the heart. This is not a literal cutting, but a divine judgment upon the thoughts, actions, and attitudes of the heart. The same is true of being beaten with many lashes. This is a symbolic way of speaking about the mental, emotional, psychological, and spiritual anguish and shame that a servant of Jesus will feel at His return when they realize how much unbelief they had and how poorly they behaved. The phrase is paired in Matthew 24:51 with "weeping and gnashing of teeth" which is an identical concept. It refers to great shame and regret before Jesus; not to punishment and torture forever in hell.[12]

So Luke 12:42-48 uses the adjective believing/unbelieving to show the importance of ongoing faith that Jesus will return soon. Yes, this ongoing faith helps guide and direct a person's behavior, but their behavior is primarily guided by whether or not they have obtained wisdom. Either way, it is critically important to note that even when a servant stops believing right truths or behaving in wise ways, they still remain a servant. To be the servant God wants and desires, we are expected to continue to believe and to behave in ways that match who we are in Him.

JOHN 3:16

For God so loved the world that He gave His only begotten Son, that whoever be-

---

[12] For a more detailed explanation, see my book, *Am I Going to Hell?* (Dallas, OR: Redeeming Press, 2019).

lieves in Him should not perish but have
everlasting life.

John 3:16 is the most famous verse in the Bible. There is good reason for this, since it contains the central invitation of the Gospel, that whoever believes in Jesus receives everlasting life. This is the clear and simple offer of the Gospel, and is what Jesus Himself consistently promised when He spoke about eternal life to others. Eternal life is freely given by God to anyone and everyone who simply and only believes in Jesus for it (cf. John 5:24; 6:47).

Yet although the promise of eternal life to all who believe in Jesus is simple to understand, it is not easy to believe. This is why the term "easy believism" is a misnomer. Yes, eternal life is freely given to those who believe in Jesus, but relatively few actually believe this! Even many who operate under the banner of "Christianity" deny that eternal life is by "faith alone in Jesus Christ alone." They argue instead that eternal life and entrance into heaven is earned through submission to the Lordship of Jesus Christ, perseverance in good works, and a life of ongoing obedience to the commands of God. Most people, even many Christians, find it hard to believe that eternal life is absolutely free to all who believe in Jesus for it.

But there are numerous, easier beliefs that can help persuade and convince us to believe in Jesus Christ *alone* for eternal life. The more we learn about God, ourselves,

Scripture, and Jesus, the more we come to understand why eternal life must be a free gift from God. If eternal life was anything other than a free gift from God, no human would be able to earn or achieve it. So the more truths we come to believe from Scripture, the easier it becomes to believe in Jesus for eternal life.[13]

Faith is a bit like a snowball. It builds as it rolls. The more we believe about Jesus, the more we end up believing about Jesus. And somewhere along the way, a person comes to discover that Jesus promises eternal life to anyone who believes in Him for it. When this truth is presented, a person either believes it, or they don't. If they believe it, then they have eternal life. Jesus guarantees it. If they don't believe it, then all is not lost. They simply need to keep moving forward, learning more about Jesus, until they come to the place where they know that Jesus fulfills what He promises. When they believe this, they will also come to believe that they have eternal life through Jesus.

Do you believe in Jesus for eternal life? If so, then eternal life is yours. If not, what is holding you back?

JOHN 6:28-29

*Then they said to Him, "What shall we
do, that we may work the works of God?"*

[13] In my book, *The Gospel According to Scripture,* I discuss several "Preparation Truths" which help convince a person to believe in Jesus Christ for eternal life. This book is forthcoming.

> *Jesus answered and said to them, "This is*
> *the work of God, that you believe in Him*
> *who He sent."*

This text has been used in various ways. Some point to this text to show that faith is indeed a work. Some of the people who were following Jesus asked what they could do to do the work of God, and Jesus tell them that the work of God is to believe in Him. This seems to imply that faith is a work, and therefore, eternal life would be gained by a work, namely, the work of faith.

Others use this verse to teach that faith is a gift from God in the mind of the believer. They teach that faith is not something that comes from the mind of a person, but is rather given by God to the person so that they might believe. John MacArthur, for example, wrongly assuming that faith is a work, says that faith cannot be "merely a human work, but a gracious work of God in us."[14]

But a careful look at the text reveals that Jesus was teaching something else entirely. In the immediately preceding context, Jesus told some of His followers that they should "not labor for the food which perishes, but for the food which endures to everlasting life" (John 6:27). Hearing Jesus talk about labor, some of the Jewish people asked what works they can do for God. Notice that they change the wording a bit, and ask Jesus

[14] John MacArthur, *The Gospel According to Jesus: What Does Jesus Mean When He Says "Follow Me"?*, Rev. and exp. ed. (Grand Rapids: Zondervan, 1994), 33.

about *works,* plural. As good Jewish people, they are thinking about pleasing God through the works of the law.[15] Jesus, however, changed it back to how He meant it, and refers to the singular *work,* and then explains what this work is. Jesus basically explains that the "work, or action, that God desires, is believing in His Son, the Lord Jesus Christ."[16]

But this does not mean that faith is a work which God performs on our behalf. Though Jesus did use the image of laboring for God, He elsewhere uses the images of *drinking* living water and *eating* the bread of life (John 4:13-14; 6:51). But nobody wonders what we should drink and eat in order to gain eternal life. Instead, people recognize that these are images Jesus used to illustrate His point about believing in Him. It is exactly the same with His image of laboring for food which endures (John 6:27). Jesus is not teaching that people have to labor for eternal life any more than He is saying that people have to drink and eat for eternal life And just as it makes no sense to say that "God eats and drinks for us because we cannot eat and drink on our own," so also, we cannot say that "God works for us because we cannot do the work of God on our own." All

[15] Most Jewish teachers did not believe that eternal life could be earned through works. But they did believe that the works of the law were pleasing to God.

[16] Bob Wilkin, "The Free Grace Position Should Rightfully Hold Claim to the Title Lordship Salvation," *Grace in Focus Newsletter* (2010). https://faithalone.org/magazine/y2010/10F1.html Last Accessed April 8, 2018.

of these pictures are ways of speaking about receiving Jesus Christ and eternal life by faith alone.

So Jesus is not saying that faith is a work, or even that faith is a work of God performed in the human heart. Instead, by saying that the work God wants is for people to believe in Him. Jesus was saying that the work that God desires is not work at all, but is the opposite of works, which is faith (cf. Rom 4:4-5; Eph 2:8-9). God does not want us to "do" anything for Him, for He has already done everything for us. He simply wants people to believe in Jesus for eternal life, thereby recognizing that everything which needs to be done has been done in Jesus.

JOHN 11:25-26

Jesus said to her, "I am the resurrection and the life. He who believes in Me, though he may die, he shall live. And whoever lives and believes in Me shall never die. Do you believe this?"

John 11:20-27 contains an excellent example of the spreadsheet of faith analogy that was used previously in this book to illustrate how faith works. Lazarus has just died, and Jesus goes to Bethany to grieve with Mary and Martha. When Jesus arrives, Martha comes out to meet Him on the road and says, "Lord, if you had been here, my brother would not have died" (John 11:21).

Jesus responded by saying, "Your brother will rise again" (John 11:23).

So Mary says, "I know that he will rise again in the resurrection at the last day" (John 11:24).

Each of these statements is a factual statement that exists on Martha's spreadsheet of beliefs. She believes that if Jesus had been present, Lazarus would not have died. Remember, they sent word to Jesus when Lazarus was sick, but He delayed in going to them until after Lazarus had died. So Martha is chiding Jesus a bit. She believes that Lazarus died because Jesus didn't show up when she wanted Him to.

But then Jesus makes another factual statement. He says, "Your brother will rise again." Now, does Martha believe this? She does. For she goes on to say, "Yes, I know, I believe, I agree that he will rise again ... but on the future day of resurrection."

Based on these beliefs, Jesus goes on to teach her some new ideas about Himself. He makes some factual statements to see if they are turned "On" or "Off" in her spreadsheet of beliefs. Jesus says, "I am the resurrection and the life. He who believes in Me, though he may die, he shall live. And whoever lives and believes in Me shall never die" (John 11:25-26).

In these verses, Jesus makes three factual statements. Each one is a truth claim about Jesus, and each one is dependent upon the other two and dependent upon what Martha has already stated about the resurrection.

Jesus is inviting her to build upon her previous beliefs and add some new beliefs to them. Jesus claims that (1) Resurrection and life reside in Him, (2) that those who die in Him will also live in Him, and (3) that who live and believe in Him will never die.

After Jesus makes these three factual statements, He says, "Do you believe this?"

Notice how Martha responds. She doesn't say, "Yes, Lord, I believe these three things. I believe that (1) Resurrection and life reside in You, (2) that those who die in You will also live in You, and (3) that who live and believe in You will never die." She does not restate the beliefs and affirm her agreement with them. Instead, she says something that has confused a lot of people over the years. She says, "Yes, Lord, I believe that You are the Christ, the Son of God, who is to come into the world."

Lots of people read these words and get confused. They see Martha state her agreement with Jesus, but then she seems to say something back to Him that is not a restatement of what Jesus just said. In other words, though she agrees, she doesn't state her agreement by summarizing what Jesus just said; instead, she states her agreement by stating her belief in something else entirely. So some people read these words from Martha and say, "Maybe to believe that Jesus is the resurrection and the life is the exact same as believing that Jesus is the Christ, the Son of God."

And while we could say that the two concepts are related, the two concepts are not identical beliefs. That is, to say that Jesus is the Christ is not the same thing as saying that Jesus is the resurrection and the life. We know this for a variety of reasons. There are lots of people in the days of Jesus who believed that He was the Christ, but did not believe that He could raise people from the dead, or even that He Himself would be raised from the dead. Furthermore, there were many people throughout biblical history who were considered to be "Messiahs" or "Christs" (that is, Deliverers, Saviors), but nobody ever thought that these people could raise others from death.

So since believing that Jesus is the Christ is not the same thing as believing that Jesus is the resurrection and the life, why does Martha answer the way she does? She answers the way she does because she is saying that *because* she believes that Jesus is the Christ, she trusts and accepts whatever else Jesus says, including these recent three statements about the resurrection.

To put it another way, Jesus makes three truth claims about Himself and then asks Martha if she believes what He has said. These are new ideas to her, and she has never been told these ideas before. So she can either accept, acknowledge, and agree with what Jesus has just said, thereby believing His words, or she can disagree with Him, thereby not believing.

But since Martha already knows and believes something else on her spreadsheet of faith, namely, that Jesus is the Christ, the Messiah, the son of God, this therefore causes Martha to realize that everything Jesus says can be trusted and accepted. Therefore, because of her belief in Jesus as the Christ, Martha also believes these new statements about Jesus, that He is the resurrection and the life, that those who die in Him will live again, and that those who live in Him will never die.

This is the Excel spreadsheet of faith at work. A cell on her spreadsheet of faith which said "Jesus is the Christ" was turned "On." As a result of this cell, another cell on her spreadsheet of faith which said, "Everything Jesus says is true" was also turned "On." So when Jesus comes along and says something she has never heard or thought of before, and then Jesus asks her if she believes these new ideas, it does not take her long to turn these cells on as well. She didn't fully understand the ramifications of what Jesus was saying, but she did know that Jesus was saying it, and that because He was the Christ, His words could always be trusted and believed. So she believed Him.

Then, of course, to provide further support and proof that her belief in Him was well-founded, Jesus went and raised Lazarus from death.

This is just one example of how the network of beliefs that exists on our spreadsheet of faith works together to consider new ideas and incorporate new beliefs.

We see it work very quickly with Martha, but it doesn't always move this fast. Sometimes the process is much slower. But regardless, this example of faith in Martha helps us understand how faith works, and how we consider and accept the various truth claims that bombard us each and every day.

Each belief is built upon others that we might or might not have on our network of faith. Faith is a vast network of individual beliefs that are constantly moving, shifting, changing, and developing over time. It is not something to be afraid of, but can be enjoyed and anticipated as we continue to follow Jesus wherever He leads.

JOHN 20:31

> *... but these are written that you may believe that Jesus is the Christ, the Son of God, and that believing you may have life in His name.*

Near the end of his Gospel account, the Apostle John provides the purpose statement for his book. He says that while he could have included many other additional signs and teachings of Jesus in the account, he specifically chose the ones he wrote down because they would help a person believe in Jesus, so that those who believed would have eternal life.

This truth from John fits perfectly with what we have learned about faith. Faith occurs when we are persuaded that something is true. Humans are persuaded by a wide variety of factors, one of which is reading about historical events of the past (cf. Luke 1:1-4). The signs in the Gospel of John are provided to persuade people about the truth regarding Jesus. Specifically, the signs cause people to believe in Jesus for eternal life.[17] Therefore, the Gospel of John is a perfect place to see that faith is persuasion. The concluding purpose of the book, recorded in John 20:30-31, brings this out quite clearly. The signs were written so that those who read them might believe (be persuaded) that Jesus is the Christ, and that through such belief (or persuasion), they might have life in His name.

Once again, we see how believing one thing can lead to believing other related truths. The Apostle John specifically chose to record several historical and miraculous signs which provide proof that Jesus was the Messiah. When we believe this, we will then come to believe that Jesus was telling the truth whenever He spoke. And if we believe this, then we can know the truth of what He taught, that anyone who believed in Him would have everlasting life. Believing in what John has written about Jesus leads a person to believe that Jesus was the Messiah, which leads a person to believe what Jesus taught, and therefore, believe in Jesus for eternal life.

---

[17] John H. Niemelä, "The Cross in John's Gospel" *JOTGES* (Spring 2003), 27.

ACTS 6:7

Then the word of God spread, and the
number of the disciples multiplied greatly
in Jerusalem, and a great many of the
priests were obedient to the faith.

Acts 6:7 has sometimes been used to defend the idea that faith is a work, or that true faith leads to a life of ongoing obedience and works. But Acts 6:7 includes the article "the" in front of the word faith, indicating that "the Christian faith" is in view rather than "faith" itself. In context, "the Christian faith" is set in contrast to "the Jewish faith" which the priests had formerly believed and practiced.

This articular use of faith does not primarily refer to believing a particular truth, but instead refers to the entire set of beliefs and behaviors that distinguish one "religion" from another. So while these priests had formerly been part of the Jewish faith, they had now converted to the Christian faith. So while "the faith" does include an element of conduct or behavior, and thus it can be spoken of as "obedience," this does not mean that "faith" itself involves works of any kind. Faith is not a work and does not necessarily lead to works.

There are numerous other passages in the New Testament which speak of "the faith" and all of them can be understood in a similar fashion (cf. Acts 13:8; 14:22; 16:5; Rom 1:5; 1 Cor 16:13; 2 Cor 13:5; Gal 1:23; 3:23; 6:10; Eph 4:13; Php 1:25-27; Col 1:23; 1 Tim

3:9-4:6; 5:8; 6:10, 21; 2 Tim 2:18; 3:8; 4:7; Titus 1:13;
Jude 3).

ACTS 13:48

*Now when the Gentiles heard this, they
were glad and glorified the word of the
Lord. And as many as had been appointed to eternal life believed.*

Some use Acts 13:48 to teach that God chooses who
will receive eternal life, and then gives faith to those
whom He has chosen. So while this verse is often used
in defense of the Reformed teaching on election and
predestination, those teachings are intricately connected
with the idea that faith is a gift from God. Acts 13:48 is
used to defend both ideas.

However, this entire understanding depends on a
dubious interpretation of the Greek word *tetagmenoi,*
which is sometimes translated as "had been appointed."
This word is a perfect participle, which can be understood in either the middle or passive voice. The phrase
"had been appointed" reveals the passive interpretation.
In this interpretation, the Gentiles are passive recipients
of faith. But the Greek participle could also be understood in the middle voice, in which case, the Greek
word could be translated as "marshalled themselves,

prepared themselves, or disposed themselves."[18] If this is the preferred translation, the Gentiles were not passive in receiving faith, but prepared themselves to believe.

But how can we decide which translation is preferable? The answer, as always, is to look at the context. In the immediate context, those who end up believing Paul and Barnabas had attended the synagogue on the Sabbath, heard the preaching of Paul, and then joined with the Jews in inviting Paul to speak a second Sabbath. The reason these Gentiles joined the Jews is because they were God-fearing proselytes (cf. Acts 13:42-43). After hearing Paul on this second Sabbath, many of these Gentiles believed what they heard.

The implication in Acts 13:48 is that these Gentile proselytes had been thinking and mulling over what Paul had said for an entire week, and after hearing him a second time, became convinced of the truth of his words. Their belief was no passive working of God on their hearts and minds, but was their week-long consideration and response to what God was doing in their midst. By the time they heard the gospel on the second Sabbath, they had disposed or prepared themselves to believe the message.

[18] Henry Alford, *The Greek New Testament and Exegetical and Critical Commentary* (Cambridge: Deighton, Bell, 1976), II:153; Robert Shank, *Elect in the Son; A Study of the Doctrine of Election* (Springfield, MO: Westcott, 1970), 87. Cf. J. Gresham Machen, *New Testament Greek for Beginners* (Upper Saddle River, NJ: Prentice Hall, 1923), 186; Richard Rackham, *The Acts of the Apostles: An Exposition* (Eugene, OR: Wipf & Stock, 2003), 221.

This understanding also fits with the broader context in several ways. First, "Acts 13 is a study in contrasts in how different people *prepare themselves* to hear the gospel."[19] In the beginning of the chapter, the contrast is between Bar-Jesus and Sergius Paulus. One man was open to the truth while the other was full of deceit (cf. Acts 13:7, 10). Then when Luke writes about Paul preaching in Pisidian Antioch, he shows how the Gentiles accept what is preached while the Jews oppose it. This event in Acts 13 marks the beginning of the theme in Acts where the Gentiles often respond favorably to the gospel while the Jews do not.[20]

The reason for this transition, Luke indicates, is not because God has now "chosen" the Gentiles instead of His other "chosen" people, the Jews, but because the Gentiles were more open to hearing, considering, examining, and accepting the things Paul preached to them, while the Jews were more set in their traditional ways and beliefs and so were less willing to consider that they might be wrong. Furthermore, the text uses the middle voice for the word "reject" (Gk., *apōtheō*) in Acts 13:46, showing that the Jewish people *themselves* rejected the message of Paul. This too was not a passive rejection foreordained or predetermined by God. Therefore, if

[19] Shawn Lazar, "Election for Baptists," *Grace in Focus Newsletter* (September-October 2014), 6.

[20] Cf. comments by Laurence M. Vance, *The Other Side of Calvinism* (Pensacola, FL: Vance Publications, 1999), 346-348.

the Jewish rejection was not passive, then neither was the Gentile acceptance.

Finally, this understanding of *tetagmenoi* as "disposed" fits best with other uses of the same term in Acts. Aside from Acts 13:48, the word is also used in Acts 15:2, 22:10, and 28:23. In Acts 15:2 and 28:23, the word is clearly referring to the actions, attitudes, and decisions of people, rather than to some divinely-ordained predisposition to the gospel which was unconditionally granted by God. Outside of the book of Acts, Luke (who also wrote Acts) uses the word in Luke 7:8 to refer to human authority and control. Paul follows a similar track when he uses this word in 1 Corinthians 16:15 to write about Christians who have devoted themselves to a particular ministry.

So although it is absolutely true that God may arrange historical events which allow a person to hear the message of the gospel, and while God definitely gives eternal life upon those who believe, God does not give the gift of faith to passive recipients. Faith is not a gift or a work. But we can be disposed, or prepared, to believe by what we learn, study, and think.

ROMANS 3:21-26

But now the righteousness of God apart from the law is revealed, being witnessed by the Law and the Prophets, even the righteousness of God, through faith in Je-

sus Christ, to all and on all who believe.
For there is no difference; for all have
sinned and fallen short of the glory of
God, being justified freely by His grace
through the redemption that is in Christ
Jesus, whom God set forth as a propitia-
tion by His blood, through faith, to
demonstrate His righteousness, because in
His forebearance God had passed over the
sins that were previously committed, to
demonstrate at the present time His
righteousness, that He might be just and
the justifier of the one who has faith in
Jesus.

This text is one of the many from Paul which reveals the similar message we learned from Jesus, that eternal life is by faith alone in Jesus Christ alone. However, Paul doesn't mention "eternal life" but rather the "righteousness of God." The two concepts are related. Since eternal life is God's life, and since we gain God's righteousness when we share His life, the terms "eternal life" and "righteousness of God" are close synonyms in Scripture. While Jesus speaks of eternal life, Paul writes of justification and the righteousness of God (and while Jesus speaks of the Kingdom of God, Paul tends to write about salvation). So while Jesus teaches that God gives eternal life to those who believe in Jesus for it, Paul similarly teaches that God gives His righteousness to all who believe in Jesus. This is what he teaches three times in these verses.

It is also crucial to recognize what Paul says about the death of Jesus in this passage. Paul writes that in previous eras, God passed over the sins that people committed. Why? According to Paul, the violent death of Jesus on the cross reveals that just as God freely forgave us by His grace for committing the greatest sin of all, which was the sin of accusing and killing His Own Son, so also, God freely forgave the sins that were previously committed. God freely forgives because God is a gracious God. God clearly and irrefutably demonstrated this by extending forgiveness to us for the crucifixion of Jesus.

So from this text we see many of the truths about faith come together. Paul uses reason and logic to show why his readers should believe in Jesus for God's righteousness. He points to the teachings of the Law and the Prophets as containing persuasive evidence that God has always invited people to receive His righteousness by faith. Paul points out that anyone and everyone is able to believe, and that faith is not a work because we are justified freely by God's grace. And these verses are really only introductory for the themes that Paul goes on to discuss in the following chapters. In Romans 4–6, Paul provides many historical, biblical, and logical proofs for why his readers should believe in Jesus for God's righteousness. These chapters, and the proofs they contain, show that in Paul's thinking, belief occurs when we are persuaded by the evidence provided.

ROMANS 4:4-5

*Now to him who works, the wages are
not counted as grace but as debt. But to
him who does not work but believes on
Him who justifies the ungodly, his faith is
accounted for righteousness.*

Romans 4:4-5 clearly refutes the idea that faith is a work. After all, if faith was a work (even a work of God), or included any form of human effort or merit, then Romans 4:4-5 would be gibberish. If faith was a work, or included works of some sort, Paul would be saying that God gives His righteousness "to him who does not work but who has the work of faith." This makes no sense. Paul is clearly contrasting faith and works, showing that one has nothing to do with the other.

Paul proceeds in the following context to show that this has always been true throughout time, so that even Abraham, the father of faith, received the righteousness of God by faith before he ever obeyed God's laws or was even circumcised (Rom 4:9-25). Good works performed *before* a person believes do not help a person achieve God's righteousness, and good works performed *after* a person believes do not help them keep God's righteousness. We must not make good works a condition for receiving eternal life, keeping eternal life, or proving that we have eternal life, for the righteousness of God is gained by faith alone in Jesus Christ alone from first to last.

ROMANS 10:17

So then faith comes by hearing, and hearing by the word of God.

Romans 10:17 shows that faith is persuasion. Paul writes that faith comes by hearing, and hearing by the Word of God. The word for *hearing* refers not just to understanding what is read or taught from Scripture, but to understanding, thinking, knowing, reasoning, and assenting to what Scripture says. As people read, study, and hear the Word of God, it works upon their hearts and minds to persuade them of the truth (cf. Gal 3:2). This is why it is so important to use Scripture when sharing the gospel. It is the Word of God that is living and active (Heb 4:12) and through which the Holy Spirit works to draw all people to Jesus Christ.

So faith is not a human work, and neither is it a work of God in the human heart. Faith rises in the human mind as a person hears, understands, and agrees with what Scripture says. Some people may need to understand more and some less, but there can be no faith without hearing and understanding.

2 CORINTHIANS 13:5

*Examine yourselves as to whether you are
in the faith. Test yourselves. Do you not
know yourselves, that Jesus Christ is in
you?—unless indeed you are disqualified.*

Second Corinthians 13:5 is often used by those who
teach that if a Christian does not have the proper type
or amount of beliefs and behaviors, then there is a good
chance that this person is not actually a Christian.
Those who hold this view call on others to examine
themselves to see whether or not they are actually a
Christian. They call on others to test themselves to see
whether or not they have actually believed and whether
or not they have the requisite amount of good works to
prove that they are a "true" Christian. If not, then such
a person should try harder, work longer, and obey more
so that they can prove the reality of their faith and genuineness of their conversion.

But since faith is not a work and does not include
works, what does this verse mean? This is once again an
"articular" use of "the faith." Paul is not telling the Corinthians to question whether or not they have really
believed, but is telling them to question whether or not
their beliefs and behaviors line up with "the Christian
faith" and what Paul himself taught and practiced when
he was among them. Paul is not saying, "Make sure you
are really a Christian," but is instead saying, "*Since you*

are a Christian, make sure your beliefs and behaviors match how Christians should believe and behave."

Paul is *not* saying that if the beliefs and behaviors of the Corinthian Christians do not line up with the proper beliefs and behaviors of "the Christian faith" then this means that they are not really Christians. No, it just means that their life and theology does not line up with who they really are.

Paul repeatedly and consistently throughout his letter affirms that the Corinthians are believers and have the righteousness of God. As a result, based on this certain reality, Paul calls them to live in light of who they actually are (cf. 1:24; 3:3; 6:14-15; 7:1; 8:9; 13:11). This is also what Paul means in 13:5. He affirms that they are his brethren in Christ, and on the basis of this affirmation, invites them to check their beliefs and behaviors to see whether or not they conform to "the [Christian] faith" (cf. the nearly identical use of "the faith" in Col 1:23).

The reference to being "disapproved" also has nothing to do with eternal life or going to heaven, but is instead about Paul's apostolic ministry. Some in Corinth were claiming that Paul's ministry was invalid. Paul brilliantly counters this argument by saying that if his ministry is disqualified, then everyone in Corinth is also disqualified for ministry, because they only became Christians through his ministry among them. But if their ministry is valid, then this proves that his is valid as well (cf. 13:3-7; 1 Cor 9:2).

EPHESIANS 2:8-9

For by grace you have been saved through faith, and that not of yourselves; it is the gift of God, not of works, lest anyone should boast.

Ephesians 2:8-9 is one of the key passages which is sometimes used to defend the idea that faith is a gift from God. For example, R. C. Sproul, in his book, *What is Faith?* writes this:

> What is meant by "not your own doing"? Is it grace or is it faith? According to all the rules of Greek grammar, there is only one possible answer to that question. In the grammatical structure of the text, the antecedent of the word *this* is the word *faith*. [21]

Strangely, Sproul provides no grammatical evidence for his assertion, and indeed, the Greek grammar of Ephesians 2:8-9 reveals exactly the opposite of what Sproul writes. [22]

[21] R. C. Sproul, *What is Faith?* (Orlando: Reformation Trust, 2010), 53.

[22] For a detailed analysis of the Greek Grammar, see René Lopez, "Is Faith a Gift from God or a Human Exercise?" *Bibliotheca Sacra 164* (July–September 2007): 266-274. http://www.dts.edu/ download/publications/bibliotheca/BibSac-Lopez-IsFaithAGiftfrom GodoraHumanExercise.pdf Last Accessed July 13, 2014.

In the preceding context, Paul is referring to what God has done for humans in Jesus Christ (Eph 2:1-7). After writing that while we were dead in trespasses (Eph 2:1-4), God made us alive together with Jesus Christ (2:5; which is a preview of 2:11-22), Paul states the main theme: "by grace you have been saved" (2:5). Paul repeats this theme in Ephesians 2:8 while adding to it the element of faith. It is in 2:8 that he also writes that "it is the gift of God."

But what is the gift of God? To what does the phrase "and *that* not of yourselves, *it* is the gift of God" refer? In other words, what is it that did not come from us humans, but came from God as a gift? Some argue that "it" is faith. And indeed, from the English, this would make sense as pronouns usually refer to their nearest antecedent. If I say, "The monkey ate the apple, and it was a gift from the zookeeper," the rules of English grammar dictate that the word "it" refers to the apple rather than the monkey. But this is not the case with Greek.

All Greek words have gender: masculine, feminine, and neuter. When a relative pronoun is used, it always agrees with the gender of the noun to which it refers. The word "faith" in Greek is feminine, and so if Paul wanted to write that faith was not of ourselves but was a gift of God, he would have used a feminine relative pronoun for the word "that" (the word "it" is not actually in the Greek). But Paul did not use the feminine version of the word "that." Instead, he used a neuter (neutral) pronoun. Therefore, it is grammatically impossible for the word "that" to refer to "faith."

The problem is that there is no neuter noun in the preceding context. So what was Paul referring to, if not to faith? It is not faith itself, but the entire "salvation package" that Paul is writing about in Ephesians 2. The description of Paul about what God has provided to us in Jesus contains a mixture of masculine and feminine nouns. So Paul uses a neuter pronoun to refer to the entire "salvation package." If God did not reveal the truth to us about human sin, we never would have realized it on our own (Eph 2:1-4). But God did reveal the truth to us, through the work of Jesus Christ, and especially the death of Jesus Christ on the cross (Eph 2:13). As a result of this revelation in Jesus, we can live free from the sin that separates us from each other, and live in love and unity instead (Eph 2:11-22). All of this is the gift of God. If, therefore, we believe what has been revealed to us through Jesus, then we will be saved from the problem of sin that has enslaved humanity since the foundation of the world.

In light of this overall context, we discover that Paul is not writing in Ephesians 2 about how people can receive eternal life or go to heaven when they die. The word "saved" in Ephesians 2:8-9 does not refer to eternal life or our eternal destiny. Instead, Paul's overall point in Ephesians 2 is about how God solved the problem of human division and strife that is caused by racial, religious, and political differences (Eph 2:1-4). Paul shows how God revealed the problem and the solution through the crucifixion of Jesus (Eph 2:5-10) so that we can all live in peace and unity with one another in this life (Eph 2:11-22), as God has always wanted and desired.

So faith is not the gift of God. The gift of God is His revelation to humanity and the salvation which comes to us by His grace. When we see, understand, and believe what God has revealed to us and done for us through the life, death, resurrection, and exaltation of Jesus, it is then that the peace of God starts to become a reality in our life here and now. It is then that all who were formerly at enmity with each other are fitted together to grow into the holy temple in the Lord, as a dwelling place of God in the Spirit (Eph 2:21-22). This is the mystery of the church, which Paul goes on to explain in Ephesians 3–4. All of this is the gift of God, and when we receive it by faith, we begin to experience this new reality in this life and on this earth.

COLOSSIANS 1:23

… if indeed you continue in the faith,
grounded and steadfast, and are not
moved away from the hope of the gospel
which you heard, which was preached to

every creature under heaven, of which I,
Paul, became a minister.

Although Colossians 1:23 is frequently cited by some teachers as proof that a failure to persevere in faith will cause someone to lose their eternal life or will prove that we were never justified in the first place, this is once again a text that can be clarified by recognizing that "*the* faith" is in view, rather than "faith." As with all the other references to "the faith" in the New Testament, the terms points to "the beliefs and behaviors that constitute Christianity" rather than to faith in Jesus for eternal life.

It is entirely possible for a person to receive eternal life through faith in Jesus, but then to later fall away from "the faith" and abandon Christianity. Such a person still has eternal life, but they no longer believe and behave the way they should. What happens to such a person? In the context, Paul explains that those who continue in "the faith" will receive a better presentation before Jesus Christ than those who do not.[23]

A time is coming when all Christians will stand before the Judgment Seat of Christ to answer for the things done in the body (2 Cor 5:10). Those who faithfully followed and served Jesus will receive additional blessing and honor from Him (cf. 1 Cor 3:12-17). When we stand before the Judgment Seat of Christ, this does not determine our eternal destiny, but only our

[23] Bob Wilkin succinctly defends this position in "Is Perseverance Required for Holy Presentation?" *Grace in Focus Newsletter* 19:1 (Jan/Feb 2004).

eternal reward. So Paul encourages the Colossian Christians to continue in the beliefs and behaviors of "the faith" which he had declared to them so that they might be presented as holy, blameless, and above reproach in His sight at the Judgment Seat of Christ.[24]

1 TIMOTHY 5:8

But if anyone does not provide for his own, and especially for those of his household, he has denied the faith and is worse than an unbeliever.

This passage is easily understood when it is recognized that Paul is referring "the [Christian] faith" rather than to *belief* itself. And this is important to recognize, for if Paul were writing here about what was necessary to receive eternal life, he would be teaching that eternal life can be lost if a person does not properly take care of their family.

Yet it is indeed possible for a Christian to have eternal life while failing to take care of his or her family. Everybody is aware of families like this. You might even come from one. But when a Christian lives in such a neglectful way, this does not mean that they are not really a Christian, or don't really believe in Jesus. Instead, their neglectful behavior simply means that they are fail-

[24] Cf. Bob Wilkin, "Is Continuing in the Faith a Condition of Eternal Life? Colossians 1:21-21" https://faithalone.org/ magazine/y1991/91march3.html Last Accessed December 29, 2018.

ing to follow the teachings and traditions of the Christian faith about the importance of loving and providing for our family members. "Part of the Christian faith—the teachings of Christianity—is to honor your parents. To neglect one's widowed mother by not taking care of her would be to deny what Christianity teaches."[25]

Some might argue that Paul's phrase at the end of this verse indicates that he does indeed have eternal destinies in mind. After all, he says that if a person doesn't take care of their family, they are "worse than an unbeliever." But this phrase doesn't mean that those Christians who fail to provide for their families will end up in hell. It means that even most unbelievers take care of their families, and so Christians who don't are behaving in worse ways than non-Christians. While Christians should be leading the way in how to love and provide for our families, when a Christian fails in this regard, their behavior is worse than that of unbelievers (cf. 1 Cor 5:1; Titus 1:13).

JAMES 2:14-26

> *What does it profit, my brethren, if someone says he has faith but does not have works? Can faith save him? … You believe that there is one God. You do well. Even the demons believe—and tremble!*

[25] Ken Yates, "Denying the Faith?" *Grace in Focus Newsletter* (Jan/Feb 2018), 8.

*... For as the body without the spirit is
dead, so faith without works is dead (Jas
2:14, 19, 26).*

James 2:14-26 has needlessly caused much angst and strife throughout the years. It has been used to teach that true faith will always result in a life of good works, so that if a person does not have the required amount of good works, this means they don't really have faith. "True faith is an active faith," people will say. "While we are saved by faith alone, we are not saved by a faith that is alone. We are not saved by faith plus works, but by a faith that works. If you claim to have faith, but don't have works, then you have dead faith, which is a spurious, false, non-existent faith." Similarly, when someone teaches or writes that eternal life is by faith alone in Jesus Christ alone, there will nearly always be someone who objects by saying that "even the demons believe."

But James 2:14-26 teaches *none* of these ideas. James 2 does not disagree with Jesus or with Paul that eternal life is by grace alone through faith alone in Jesus Christ alone. When we take everything we have learned about faith in this book and apply it to James 2, we discover the beautiful truths of this text and how the message of James fits perfectly with the message of Jesus and Paul. Three key insights about this text reveal what James is teaching.

First, eternal life is not in view. James is not writing his letter to tell people how to receive eternal life, or even how to know they have eternal life. Instead, James is writing this letter to deal with some practical issues that have arisen in the church and to tell Christians how to handle them in a Christlike and loving way. This is a practical letter full of discipleship truths for Christians.

In many ways, this letter is quite similar to the Discipleship Manual of Jesus as found in the Sermon on the Mount (Matt 5–7). James knows his readers are Christians and wants them to live in light of their identity. He knows they are brethren and he knows they have faith (Jas 1:2-3). So this letter contains practical teaching for Christians on how to live as the family of God in this world.

James 2:14-26 must be read in light of this overall theme of the letter. James does not want his readers to question whether or not they have eternal life, or whether or not their faith is "real." Instead, James has noticed a practical and relational issue in the church and is seeking to address it. What is this issue? It is that some Christians had daily, physical needs for food and clothing (2:15), and other Christians were responding to these needs by saying, "I believe God will provide for you" (2:16). James mocks this response by saying, "What good is that?" (2:16-17).

Not even the word "save" in James 2:14 indicates that James is writing about eternal life. The word "save" always means "deliverance" and only context can determine what kind of deliverance is in view. Here, James is writing about how a person can help save his Christian brethren from hunger and nakedness (2:15). Good works can also save our relationships with other Christians (1:19-20), and save our lives from premature physical death (1:21; 5:20). Good works can save women and orphans from being mistreated and abused (cf. Jas 1:27). So good works are critically important, and good works do "save" us, but they have no place in helping us gain and keep our eternal life, or prove that we have it.

So James is saying that when someone is hungry, naked, sick, lonely, or poor, faith, by itself, is worthless. James says, "Do not tell others that God will provide for their needs ... *you* provide for their needs. Do not tell them that you will pray for them ... *do something* for them. Do not speak a word of faith that they will be clothed and fed ... *you* clothe and feed them." James is saying that faith, by itself, does not fill bellies or provide warmth. Food and clothes do that. So it is good if you believe God can provide for the needs of others. But God wants to provide for their needs through you. This is what James is teaching.

James is saying that if you want to affect change in this world, don't stop at belief; you need to *do something*. While mental, emotional, spiritual, and psychological change can occur through changing our beliefs, bringing about physical change in this world and in the lives of others requires a change in behavior. Believing and praying that God will stop war, end poverty, and rescue children from slavery does nothing to actually accomplish these tasks. If you want there to be progress in these areas, you need to get out of your prayer closet and actually start working to bring about the change you want to see.

This does not mean that faith and prayer are ineffective. It means that they are ineffective *by themselves* to accomplish change in this world. Faith and prayer are to be the catalysts that help us see the heart of God and discuss with Him how He wants us to get involved in advancing His Kingdom on earth. Faith and prayer provide the vision for how to get involved in the action of bringing heaven down to earth.

All of this is in relation to physical, worldly needs and issues. James does not have in view the spiritual need of eternal life, nor is he writing about this topic. James would agree that when it comes to the spiritual need of every person for eternal life from God, faith alone is enough, for faith is all that is needed. No amount of good works or human effort can ever achieve the righteousness of God (Jas 2:10). Eternal life is a spiritual need, and is therefore received through spiritual faith, and nothing else. James does not disagree with or modify this truth at all.

So James is not challenging whether or not people *really* believe, or whether or not their faith is *genuine.*

He is just saying that when it comes to practical, physical needs of other people, faith, by itself, accomplishes nothing.

This leads to the second critical point that helps us understand what James is saying in these verses. Many people believe that James is teaching that true faith will lead to visible actions, so that if a person doesn't have the visible actions, this means they don't have true faith. But James is actually teaching the exact opposite truth. The point of James throughout these verses is that no one can ever *see* faith in someone else. James is teaching that faith is invisible, that it cannot be seen at all. James points this out in various ways throughout this section that actions and behaviors tell us almost nothing about what a person believes.

We see this first in James 2:14 where he writes, "If someone says he has faith." He does not write, "If someone has faith." Why not? Because we cannot see whether or not a person has faith. The only indication we have that someone else has a particular belief is if they tell us they have it. There is no other way to know what beliefs another person has. The NIV translation of this phrase as "if a man *claims* to have faith" is somewhat misleading, as it gives the impression that the man doesn't actually have the faith which he claims to have. But there is no other way to know what a person believes than by them telling us what they believe. So if they tell us they have a certain belief, since it is impossible to see into their mind if they truly do have this belief, we must give them the benefit of the doubt, and believe that they know what it is that they believe.

When people hear that it is impossible to see faith, someone always objects that behaviors truly do reveal beliefs. James is aware of this objection, and gives voice to it in 2:18-19. It is obvious from the phrase "But someone will say ..." that James has introduced the objection. What is not so obvious is where the objection ends. The NKJV puts it half-way through verse 18: "You have faith, and I have works." But the NASB puts the end-quote at the end of verse 18, so that the entire verse is included in the objection. Since Greek did not have quote marks, how can we know where the quote of the objector ends?

The answer is to understand the grammatical rules of "Epistolary Diatribe." Since ancient letter-writers did not have quote marks at their disposal, they used other methods in writing their letters (epistles) to indicate when they are dialoguing with someone who disagrees (diatribe). There were three basic rules (which are not universally applied in every instance). First, the words of the objector are introduced with the verb "say" or "said" (e.g., "You have heard it said," Or "But someone will say,"). Second, when the letter-writer wants to begin his refutation of this objection, he begins by inserting an adversative conjunction (e.g., "But" or "Of course not!"). Finally, to indicate his disagreement, the letter-writer includes a gentle mocking, or name-calling, of the person being refuted (e.g., "Who are you, Oh man?" or "Oh foolish man!"). Clear examples of this "Epistolary Diatribe" can be found in Romans 9:19-20 and 1 Corinthians 15:35-36.

James 2:18-20 is also a clear example of "Epistolary Diatribe." James introduces the objector with the words, "But someone will say." And where do we see an adversative conjunction followed by a gentle name-calling? Not in the middle of verse 18, or at the beginning of verse 19, but at the beginning of verse 20. James begins his refutation of the objector in verse 20 by saying, "*But do you want to know, O foolish man* ..." This means that all of verses 18 and 19 are the words of the objector.[26]

This helps us understand the overall argument and thought flow of James. It is the objector, not James, who argues that works reveal faith. It is the objector, not James, who says that the faith of demons is clearly seen in how demons tremble in fear before God. This means that when people quote James 2:19, "Even the demons believe," they are not quoting James, but somebody who disagrees with James. James does not disagree that demons have faith. Of course demons have faith! All beings believe things, including demons. Demons believe many things about God, themselves, and humanity. And many of their beliefs are correct beliefs. Indeed, in

[26] One Bible translation which recognizes this structure is the *The Weymouth New Testament* (New York: Baker & Taylor, 1903).

the context here, the objector says that the demons believe that God is one. This is a correct belief. James believes this; I believe it; and I hope you believe it too.

Note that nobody receives eternal life by believing that God is one. God gives eternal life to those humans who believe in Jesus for it. Eternal life has not been offered to demons, and there is no indication anywhere in Scripture that they believe in Jesus for eternal life. So people who use James 2:19 as a way to oppose the biblical gospel teaching that eternal life is by faith alone in Jesus Christ alone are simply revealing that they do not understand the offer of eternal life in the gospel, what it is that James is actually teaching in this passage, or that they are quoting with approval someone who actually disagrees with James.

So in 2:20, when James sets out to refute the objector, his point is to show the opposite of what the objector argued. Since the objector argued that faith *does* reveal itself by actions, James wants to show that it does *not*. And while the objector used the central Jewish statement of faith (God is One) as "Exhibit A," James uses the central Jewish example of faith as his Exhibit A. James uses the example of Abraham, the father of faith.

In 2:21, James writes that Abraham was "justified by works when he offered Isaac his son on the altar." This is a very challenging verse for some Christians, because we have been taught that we are justified by faith, *not* by works (Rom 4:4-5). Yet James seems to say the exact opposite. The apparent contradiction is solved by noting that whenever Paul writes about Abrahams' justification by faith, he points to Abraham's justification *before God* as recorded in Genesis 15:6. But when James writes about Abraham's justification, he points to Genesis 22 where Abraham offered his son Isaac on the altar.

James is showing that while Abraham *said* he had faith in God (and indeed, Scripture says he did), no one could actually see this faith. In fact, quite often during the 25 (or more) years between his reported faith in Genesis 15 and his near-sacrifice of Isaac in Genesis 22, Abraham's actions seemed to indicate a complete lack of faith. His actions did *not* always match his "claim" to faith. But he did have faith.

So when James writes that Abraham was justified by works when he almost offered his son Isaac on the altar, he is not talking about justification by faith before God, but is talking about justification by works in the sight of men. Since humans cannot see faith, but can see actions, only actions can tell us anything about a person. For decades, Abraham had been saying that he was a friend of God, but it was only after Abraham almost sacrificed his son, and then was stopped from doing so by God, that people were able to see that Abraham truly was a friend of God (Jas 2:23). People saw his righteous actions, and so declared that he truly was righteous. He was justified by his works in the sight of other people.

Following this example, James puts the nail in the coffin of his objector's argument by using a complete opposite example. Since Abraham was the father of the Jewish faith, and was chosen by God, James shows that the same truths apply to Rahab, a female Gentile prostitute (Jas 2:25). She likely told the spies that she believed that God would hand Jericho over to them, but they had no way of seeing her faith. But she was justified by her works in their eyes when she did not hand them over to the authorities, but instead sent them out another way. Once again, faith by itself does nothing, and it cannot be seen by humans or verified by them. To actually help other people, it is works that are needed.

With all of this in mind, we now understand what James means by "dead faith" (Jas 2:19, 26). This is the third and final key which helps the meaning of James 2 become clear. Dead faith is not non-existent faith, spurious faith, fake faith, or false faith. Dead faith is ineffective faith. Dead faith is faith that exists, but doesn't *do* anything meaningful. Just like a dead body. The dead body exists, but it just lays there. It does not do what God intended bodies to do. Does a dead body exist? Yes, it does. A dead body is not a non-existent, spurious, fake, or false body. It is a real body. It simply is not functioning the way God intended or desired.

So also with faith. A dead faith is a real faith. It really exists. It is truly there. It is just unproductive and "unenergized." Just as the spirit energizes the body to help it actually *do* things in this world, so also, works energize faith to help it accomplish things in this world (Jas 2:26). While we cannot see faith, we can see actions, and should encourage people who say they have particular beliefs to energize their faith with their actions.

The person who says they have a particular belief should be praised and encouraged for having this belief. We have no reason to doubt someone when they say they believe something. If someone says they believe something, we should believe them. Since we cannot see into a person's heart or mind, and since actions do not irrefutably reveal what a person believes, if a person says they believe something, we have no good reason to doubt them.

But we have every right, says James, to remind a person that we cannot see their faith. Faith is invisible to the human eye. While faith alone is perfectly fine for receiving eternal life from God, faith by itself does nothing when it comes to interpersonal relationships and meeting human needs. So when a person says they believe that God will provide, meet a need, take care of a situation, heal, comfort, care, feed, clothe, or whatever the case may be, we can say, "It is wonderful that you believe this; but what are you going to *do* about it? I cannot see your faith, but I can see your actions, and in this situation, your actions are more beneficial than your faith."

So James does not contradict anything we have learned about faith in this book. He agrees that faith is not a work and that faith does not necessarily lead to works. He also agrees (and in fact proves) that works do not indicate anything one way or the other about a person's beliefs. Only God can see a person's heart and mind, and therefore, only God can see what a person believes. We humans can, however, see actions. This means that rather than tell people we believe that God will provide for them, or that we are praying for their needs, we should actually do something about their needs. Similarly, we must not make judgments about a person's beliefs (or their eternal destiny) based on their actions. Actions and good works are critically important for the Christian, but they do not help us gain eternal life, keep eternal life, or prove that we have eternal life.

CONCLUSION

There are many dozens of passages about faith that have not been considered in this chapter. But hopefully the sampling of texts discussed above provides a framework for how all the other texts can also be understood. And hopefully, as you have read and studied these texts on your own, you have come to be persuaded by some new ideas about faith. In other words, I hope that the evidence provided in this chapter from Scripture brought you to the place where you changed some of your beliefs about belief. This is, after all, how faith works.

CONCLUSION

This book was written in reverse. Though the first several chapters of this book presented several key truths about faith and then concluded with a chapter that considered several key biblical passages about faith, the initial study and research for this book went in the opposite direction. I originally believed something very different about faith than I do now. But as I set out to study what the Scriptures teach about faith, I uncovered some truths from the various texts that convinced and persuaded me to change my beliefs about belief. Maybe the same thing has happened with you.

But regardless of what you now believe about belief, I would like to end this book with two final exhortations.

First, no matter how you view faith, never let go of the truth that eternal life is received by grace alone through faith alone in Jesus Christ alone. This central gospel truth is a guiding light for all other truths in Scripture. Those who neglect or forsake this truth always end up traveling some strange doctrinal paths. So hold on to this truth and let your study of Scripture continually affirm and support it, for this is one of the central truths of the Bible. As you hold on to this central gospel truth, Jesus will, by His Spirit, uphold and guide you into all truth.

Second, as long as you know that you are safe and secure in the arms of Jesus, you will never need to be afraid of changing or challenging your beliefs. Knowing that you cannot ever be taken out of God's hands will give you the courage to tread where few others dare to go. You will have no fear of doubt or deception, because you know that God will keep you safe and secure. This is the only recipe for moving forward with your faith and taking the next step in your adventure with God.

So have you encountered hard questions? Ask away, knowing that God will show you the answers you seek. Do you have fears? Leap into the great unknown, trusting that God will raise you up. Do you have doubts? Embrace them, for doubt is the first step on the road to truth. Do you wonder where God is taking you? Jump into the wheelbarrow and enjoy the ride.

Faith is an adventure of the mind, and you are now set free to follow the road wherever it goes.

AFTERWORD

"Blessed assurance! Jesus is mine!"
–Fanny Crosby

Christians often will sing what they are too afraid to say.
I sincerely believe more doctrinal truth has been trans-
ferred from one generation of Christians to the next
through the songs that are sung than through the sermons that are heard or the books that are read. Fanny
Crosby's famous hymn declares, with boldness and clarity that is not common enough among Christians today,
her absolute assurance regarding her standing in Christ.
It seems some people are afraid if they allow themselves
to seem too confident in their eternal life, or if they give
others confidence of their own eternal life, then perhaps
Christians will lose their motivation for serving God.
Others fear they might become too "dogmatic," rigidly
holding to things the rest of the culture knows to be
false. Nothing could be further from the truth.

I would encourage you, reader, to go back over the short "Conclusion" section of this book one more time. Assurance of your eternal life, or to use Jeremy's expression (borrowed from another Crosby hymn), knowing you are "safe and secure in the arms of Jesus" is the starting point of spiritual growth. If you are shaky on whether or not God even accepts you, or if you fear that perhaps He might at some point cease to accept you, then all of your attempts at serving Him will be tinged with fear and frustration, rather than growing from the love, joy, and peace that comes from a life lived in the Holy Spirit.

This is where I believe the importance of this book lies. Confidence in your belief can not long endure without some understanding of what it actually means to believe. In a Christian environment where everyone seems to agree that eternal life is by faith alone, the greatest danger to a believer's assurance is a challenge to the definition of the word "faith." Many caution the questioning Christian with statements like "Sure, eternal life is by faith alone, but is what you have *actually* faith?" This book equips the believer to have a strong and satisfying answer.

It is likely, as you continue along your spiritual journey, you will be confronted with the kind of teaching Jeremy described in the early parts of the book. A well-meaning but dangerously misguided teacher will likely try to cause his hearers to avoid particular sins or to be more zealous in their service when he brings up some of the verses Jeremy mentioned in his last chapter. Especially using James 2, such teachers will suggest that perhaps your faith is not actually "real," or perhaps is not strong enough, or maybe it's the wrong "kind" of faith. Likely this will be followed by an admonition to prove the genuineness of your faith, both to others as well as to yourself, by doing certain works or by abstaining from certain sins. This is, of course, getting the cart dangerously ahead of the horse, and will inevitably lead to the frustrating experience described in Romans 7:14-24. Legalism is operating under the principle of Law. "To be acceptable to God you must do …" Grace is the opposite. Grace says all "doings" are able to be done because of the fact that you are already accepted by God. The opportunity to serve Him, as well as our being equipped to serve, are just more gifts that He is pleased to give.

So now, dear reader, having read this book you have been well-taught and are now well-equipped. When someone tries to cause you to question the validity of your faith, whether it be a human teacher or simply your own weakness of conscience, you need not be deceived. If you think that your only options are to look at your own righteousness scorecard, to look internally to see if you have been sufficiently transformed to merit assurance of a genuine faith, then you would be headed for great turmoil of soul, and likely to ineffectiveness is service.

But since you now know what faith is, you know the better solution. I admonish you, remember what you have learned. Don't look to yourself, to your zeal in service, your avoidance of particular sins, or even to the "degree" of strength of your faith. Do not look to yourself at all. Instead, look always and only to Jesus. Look at His divine power and His infinite love. Look to His finished work on the cross. It is He who is the "perfecter of your faith" (Heb 12:2), and there is no work the Holy Spirit loves to do more than to make much of Him. With your spiritual eyes on the Savior, the Giver of eternal life to all who believe, all worry about yourself fades to nothing. The more you see of Him, the more your heart will say with the apostle Paul (as you've likely sung more times than you can remember):

"I know whom I have believed, and am persuaded that he is able ..."[1]

—**Kent Young**
Contributing author at TheGracelings.com,
ThinkOutsidePolitics.com,
and SeekerOfChrist.org

---

[1] 2 Timothy 1:12, as sung in the hymn "I Know Whom I Have Believed" by D. W. Whittle.

ABOUT JEREMY MYERS

Jeremy Myers is a popular author, blogger, podcaster, and Bible teacher who lives in Oregon with his wife and three daughters. He primarily writes at RedeemingGod.com, where he seeks to help liberate people from the shackles of religion. His site also provides an online discipleship group where thousands of like-minded people discuss life and theology and encourage each other to follow Jesus into the world.

If you appreciated the content of this book, would you consider recommending it to your friends and leaving a review online? Thanks!

JOIN JEREMY MYERS AND LEARN MORE

Take Bible and theology courses by joining Jeremy at
RedeemingGod.com/join/
Receive updates about free books, discounted books, and new books by joining Jeremy at
RedeemingGod.com/read-books/

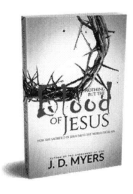

NOTHING BUT THE BLOOD OF JESUS: HOW THE SACRIFICE OF JESUS SAVES THE WORLD FROM SIN

Do you have difficulties reconciling God's behavior in the Old Testament with that of Jesus in the New?

Do you find yourself trying to rationalize God's violent demeanor in the Bible to unbelievers or even to yourself?

Does it seem disconcerting that God tells us not to kill others but He then takes part in some of the bloodiest wars and vindictive genocides in history?

The answer to all such questions is found in Jesus on the cross. By focusing your eyes on Jesus Christ and Him crucified, you come to understand that God was never angry at human sinners, and that no blood sacrifice was ever needed to purchase God's love, forgiveness, grace, and mercy.

In *Nothing but the Blood of Jesus*, J. D. Myers shows how the death of Jesus on the cross reveals the truth about the five concepts of sin, law, sacrifice, scapegoating, and bloodshed. After carefully defining each, this book shows how these definitions provide clarity on numerous biblical texts.

REVIEWS

Building on his previous book, "The Atonement of God," the work of René Girard and a solid grounding in the Scriptures, Jeremy Myers shares fresh and challenging insights with us about sin, law, sacrifice, scapegoating and blood. This book reveals to us how truly precious the blood of Jesus is and the way of escaping the cycle of blame, rivalry, scapegoating, sacrifice and violence that has plagued humanity since the time of Cain and Abel. "Nothing but the Blood of Jesus" is an important and timely literary contribution to a world desperately in need of the non-violent message of Jesus. –Wesley Rostoll

My heart was so filled with joy while reading this book. Jeremy you've reminded me once more that as you walk with Jesus and spend time in His presence, He talks to you and reveals Himself through the Scriptures. –Reader

THE ATONEMENT OF GOD: BUILDING YOUR THEOLOGY ON A CRUCIVISION OF GOD

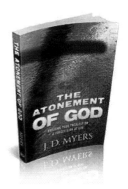

After reading this book, you will never read the Bible the same way again.

By reading this book, you will learn to see God in a whole new light. You will also learn to see yourself in a whole new light, and learn to live life in a whole new way.

The book begins with a short explanation of the various views of the atonement, including an explanation and defense of the "Non-Violent View" of the atonement. This view argues that God did not need or demand the death of Jesus in order to forgive sins. In fact, God has never been angry with us at all, but has always loved and always forgiven.

Following this explanation of the atonement, J. D. Myers takes you on a journey through 10 areas of theology which are radically changed and transformed by the Non-Violent view of the atonement. Read this book, and let your life and theology look more and more like Jesus Christ!

REVIEWS

Outstanding book! Thank you for helping me understand "Crucivision" and the "Non-Violent Atonement." Together, they help it all make sense and fit so well into my personal thinking about God. I am encouraged to be truly free to love and forgive, because God has always loved and forgiven without condition, because Christ exemplified this grace on the Cross, and because the Holy Spirit is in the midst of all life, continuing to show the way through people like you. –Samuel R. Mayer

This book gives another view of the doctrines we have been taught all of our lives. And this actually makes more sense than what we have heard. I myself have had some of these thoughts but couldn't quite make the sense of it all by myself. J.D. Myers helped me answer some questions and settle some confusion for my doctrinal views. This is truly a refreshing read. Jesus really is the demonstration of who God is and God is much easier to understand than being so mean and vindictive in the Old Testament. The tension between the wrath of God and His justice and the love of God are eased when reading this understanding of the atonement. Read with an open mind and enjoy! –Clare N. Bez

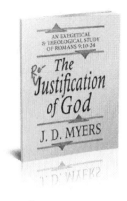

THE RE-JUSTIFICATION OF GOD: A STUDY OF ROMANS 9:10-24

Romans 9 has been a theological battleground for centuries. Scholars from all perspectives have debated whether Paul is teaching corporate or individual election, whether or not God truly hates Esau, and how to understand the hardening of Pharaoh's heart. Both sides have accused the other of misrepresenting God.

In this book, J. D. Myers presents a mediating position. Gleaning from both Calvinistic and Arminian insights into Romans 9, J. D. Myers presents a beautiful portrait of God as described by the pen of the Apostle Paul.

Here is a way to read Romans 9 which allows God to remain sovereign and free, but also allows our theology to avoid the deterministic tendencies which have entrapped certain systems of the past.

Read this book and—maybe for the first time—learn to see God the way Paul saw Him.

WHY YOU HAVE NOT COMMITTED THE UNFORGIVABLE SIN: FINDING FORGIVENESS FOR THE WORST OF SINS

Are you afraid that you have committed the unforgivable sin?

In this book, you will learn what this sin is and why you have not committed it. After surveying the various views about blasphemy against the Holy Spirit and examining Matthew 12:31-32, you will learn what the sin is and how it is committed.

As a result of reading this book, you will gain freedom from the fear of committing the worst of all sins, and learn how much God loves you!

REVIEWS

This book addressed things I have struggled and felt pandered to for years, and helped to bring wholeness to my heart again. –Natalie Fleming

A great read, on a controversial subject; biblical, historical and contextually treated to give the greatest understanding. May be the best on this subject (and there is very few) ever written. – Tony Vance

You must read this book. Forgiveness is necessary to see your blessings. So if you purchase this book, [you will have] no regrets. –Virtuous Woman

Jeremy Myers covers this most difficult topic thoroughly and with great compassion. –J. Holland

Wonderful explication of the unpardonable sin. God loves you more than you know. May Jesus Christ be with you always. –Robert M Sawin III

Excellent book! Highly recommend for anyone who has anxiety and fear about having committed the unforgivable sin. –William Tom

As someone who is constantly worried that they have disappointed or offended God, this book was, quite literally, a "Godsend." I thought I had committed this sin as I swore against the Holy Spirit in my mind. It only started after reading the verse about it in the Bible. The swear words against Him came into my mind over and over and I couldn't seem to stop no matter how much I prayed. I was convinced I was going to hell and cried constantly. I was extremely worried and depressed. This book has allowed me to breathe again, to have hope again. Thank you, Jeremy. I will read and re-read. I believe this book was definitely God inspired. I only wish I had found it sooner. –Sue

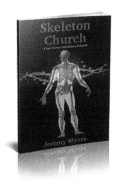

SKELETON CHURCH: A BARE-BONES DEFINITION OF CHURCH (PREFACE TO THE CLOSE YOUR CHURCH FOR GOOD BOOK SERIES)

The church has a skeleton which is identical in all types of churches. Unity and peace can develop in Christianity if we recognize this skeleton as the simple, bare-bones definition of church. But when we focus on the outer trappings—the skin, hair, and eye color, the clothes, the muscle tone, and other outward appearances—division and strife form within the church.

Let us return to the skeleton church and grow in unity once again.

REVIEWS

I worried about buying another book that aimed at reducing things to a simple minimum, but the associations of the author along with the price gave me reason to hope and means to see. I really liked this book. First, because it wasn't identical to what other simple church people are saying. He adds unique elements that are worth reading. Second, the size is small enough to read, think, and pray about without getting lost. –Abel Barba

In *Skeleton Church*, Jeremy Myers makes us rethink church. For Myers, the church isn't a style of worship, a row of pews, or even a building. Instead, the church is the people of God, which provides the basic skeletal structure of the church. The muscles, parts, and flesh of the church are how we carry Jesus' mission into our own neighborhoods in our own unique ways. This eBook will make you see the church differently. –Travis Mamone

This book gets back to the basics of the New Testament church—who we are as Christians and what our perspective should be in the world we live in today. Jeremy cuts away all the institutional layers of a church and gets to the heart of our purpose as Christians in the world we live in and how to affect the people around us with God heart and view in mind. Not a physical church in mind. It was a great book and I have read it twice now. – Vaughn Bender

The Skeleton Church ... Oh. My. Word. Why aren't more people reading this!? It was well-written, explained everything beautifully, and it was one of the best explanations of how God intended for church to be. Not to mention an easy read! The author took it all apart, the church, and showed us how it should be. He made it real. If you are searching to find something or someone to show you what God intended for the church, this is the book you need to read. –Ericka

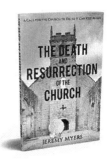

THE DEATH AND RESURRECTION OF THE CHURCH (VOLUME 1 IN THE CLOSE YOUR CHURCH FOR GOOD BOOK SERIES)

In a day when many are looking for ways to revitalize the church, Jeremy Myers argues that the church should die … so that it can rise again.

This is not only because of the universal principle that death precedes resurrection, but also because the church has adopted certain Satanic values and goals and the only way to break free from our enslavement to these values is to die.

But death will not be the end of the church, just as death was not the end of Jesus. If the church follows Jesus into death, and even to the hellish places on earth, it is only then that the church will rise again to new life and vibrancy in the Kingdom of God.

REVIEWS

I have often thought on the church and how its acceptance of corporate methods and assimilation of cultural media mores taints its mission but Jeremy Myers eloquently captures in words the true crux of the matter—

that the church is not a social club for do-gooders but to disseminate the good news to all the nooks and crannies in the world and particularly and primarily those bastions in the reign of evil. That the "gates of Hell" Jesus pronounces indicate that the church is in an offensive, not defensive, posture as gates are defensive structures.

I must confess that in reading I was inclined to be in agreement as many of the same thinkers that Myers riffs upon have influenced me also—Walter Wink, Robert Farrar Capon, Greg Boyd, NT Wright, etc. So as I read, I frequently nodded my head in agreement. –GN Trifanaff

The book is well written, easy to understand, organized and consistent thoughts. It rightfully makes the reader at least think about things as … is "the way we have always done it" necessarily the Biblical or Christ-like way, or is it in fact very sinful?! I would recommend the book for pastors and church officers; those who have the most moving-and-shaking clout to implement changes, or keep things the same. –Joel M. Wilson

Absolutely phenomenal. Unless we let go of everything Adamic in our nature, we cannot embrace anything Christlike. For the church to die, we the individual temples must dig our graves. It is a must read for all who take issues about the body of Christ seriously. –Mordecai Petersburg

PUT SERVICE BACK INTO THE CHURCH SERVICE (VOLUME 2 IN THE CLOSE YOUR CHURCH FOR GOOD BOOK SERIES)

Churches around the world are trying to revitalize their church services. There is almost nothing they will not try. Some embark on multi-million dollar building campaigns while others sell their buildings to plant home churches. Some hire celebrity pastors to attract crowds of people, while others hire no clergy so that there can be open sharing in the service.

Yet despite everything churches have tried, few focus much time, money, or energy on the one thing that churches are supposed to be doing: loving and serving others like Jesus.

Put Service Back into the Church Service challenges readers to follow a few simple principles and put a few ideas into practice which will help churches of all types and sizes make serving others the primary emphasis of a church service.

REVIEWS

Jeremy challenges church addicts, those addicted to an unending parade of church buildings, church services, Bible studies, church programs and more to follow Jesus into our communities, communities filled with lonely, hurting people and BE the church, loving the people in our world with the love of Jesus. Do we need another training program, another seminar, another church building, a remodeled church building, more staff, updated music, or does our world need us, the followers of Jesus, to BE the church in the world? The book is well-written, challenging and a book that really can make a difference not only in our churches, but also and especially in our neighborhoods and communities. –Charles Epworth

I just finished *Put Service Back Into Church Service* by Jeremy Myers, and as with his others books I have read on the church, it was very challenging. For those who love Jesus, but are questioning the function of the traditional brick and mortar church, and their role in it, this is a must read. It may be a bit unsettling to the reader who is still entrenched in traditional "church," but it will make you think, and possibly re-evaluate your role in the church. Get this book, and all others on the church by Jeremy. –Ward Kelly

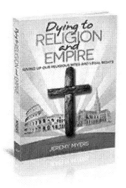

DYING TO RELIGION AND EMPIRE (VOLUME 3 IN THE CLOSE YOUR CHURCH FOR GOOD BOOK SERIES)

Could Christianity exist without religious rites or legal rights? In *Dying to Religion and Empire*, I not only answer this question with an emphatic "Yes!" but argue that if the church is going to thrive in the coming decades, we must give up our religious rites and legal rights.

Regarding religious rites, I call upon the church to abandon the quasi-magical traditions of water baptism and the Lord's Supper and transform or redeem these practices so that they reflect the symbolic meaning and intent which they had in New Testament times.

Furthermore, the church has become far too dependent upon certain legal rights for our continued existence. Ideas such as the right to life, liberty, and the pursuit of happiness are not conducive to living as the people of God who are called to follow Jesus into servanthood and death. Also, reliance upon the freedom of speech, the freedom of assembly, and other such freedoms as established by the Bill of Rights have made the church a servant of the state rather than a servant of God and the gospel. Such freedoms must be forsaken if we are going to live within the rule and reign of God on earth.

This book not only challenges religious and political liberals but conservatives as well. It is a call to leave behind the comfortable religion we know, and follow Jesus into the uncertain and wild ways of radical discipleship. To rise and live in the reality of God's Kingdom, we must first die to religion and empire.

REVIEWS

> Jeremy is one of the freshest, freest authors out there— and you need to hear what he has to say. This book is startling and new in thought and conclusion. Are the "sacraments" inviolate? Why? Do you worship at a secular altar? Conservative? Liberal? Be prepared to open your eyes. Mr. Myers will not let you keep sleeping!

> Jeremy Myers is one or the most thought provoking authors that I read, this book has really helped me to look outside the box and start thinking how can I make more sense of my relationship with Christ and how can I show others in a way that impacts them the way that Jesus' disciples impacted their world. Great book, great author. – Brett Hotchkiss

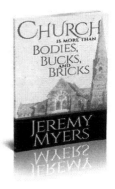

CHURCH IS MORE THAN BODIES, BUCKS, & BRICKS (VOLUME 4 IN THE CLOSE YOUR CHURCH FOR GOOD BOOK SERIES)

Many people define church as a place and time where people gather, a way for ministry money to be given and spent, and a building in which people regularly meet on Sunday mornings.

In this book, author and blogger Jeremy Myers shows that church is more than bodies, bucks, and bricks.

Church is the people of God who follow Jesus into the world, and we can be the church no matter how many people we are with, no matter the size of our church budget, and regardless of whether we have a church building or not.

By abandoning our emphasis on more people, bigger budgets, and newer buildings, we may actually liberate the church to better follow Jesus into the world.

REVIEWS

This book does more than just identify issues that have been bothering me about church as we know it, but it goes into history and explains how we got here. In this way it is similar to Viola's *Pagan Christianity*, but I found it a much more enjoyable read. Jeremy goes into more detail on the three issues he covers as well as giving a lot of practical advice on how to remedy these situations. – Portent

Since I returned from Africa 20 years ago I have struggled with going to church back in the States. This book helped me not feel guilty and has helped me process this struggle. It is challenging and overflows with practical suggestions. He loves the church despite its imperfections and suggests ways to break the bondage we find ourselves in. –Truealian

Jeremy Meyers always writes a challenging book ... It seems the American church (as a whole) is very comfortable with the way things are ... The challenge is to get out of the brick and mortar buildings and stagnant programs and minister to the needy in person with funds in hand to meet their needs especially to the widows and orphans as we are directed in the scriptures. –GGTexas

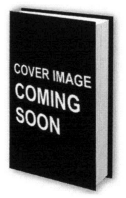

CRUCIFORM PASTORAL LEADERSHIP (VOLUME 5 IN THE CLOSE YOUR CHURCH FOR GOOD BOOK SERIES)

This book is forthcoming in early 2019.

The final volume in the *Close Your Church for Good* book series look at issues related to pastoral leadership in the church. It discusses topics such as preaching and pastoral pay from the perspective of the cross.

The best way pastors can lead their church is by following Jesus to the cross!

This book will be published in early 2019.

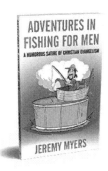

ADVENTURES IN FISHING (FOR MEN)

Adventures in Fishing (for Men) is a satirical look at evangelism and church growth strategies.

Using fictional accounts from his attempts to become a world-famous fisherman, Jeremy Myers shows how many of the evangelism and church growth strategies of today do little to actually reach the world for Jesus Christ.

Adventures in Fishing (for Men) pokes fun at some of the popular evangelistic techniques and strategies endorsed and practiced by many Christians in today's churches. The stories in this book show in humorous detail how little we understand the culture that surrounds us or how to properly reach people with the gospel of Jesus Christ. The story also shows how much time, energy, and money goes into evangelism preparation and training with the end result being that churches rarely accomplish any actual evangelism.

REVIEWS

I found *Adventures in Fishing* (*For Men*) quite funny! Jeremy Myers does a great job shining the light on some of the more common practices in Evangelism today. His allegory gently points to the foolishness that is found within a system that takes the preaching of the gospel and tries to reduce it to a simplified formula. A formula that takes what should be an organic, Spirit led experience and turns it into a gospel that is nutritionally benign.

If you have ever EE'd someone you may find Myers' book offensive, but if you have come to the place where you realize that Evangelism isn't a matter of a script and checklists, then you might benefit from this light-hearted peek at Evangelism today. –Jennifer L. Davis

Adventures in Fishing (for Men) is good book in understanding evangelism to be more than just being a set of methods or to do list to follow. –Ashok Daniel

CHRISTMAS REDEMPTION: WHY CHRISTIANS SHOULD CELEBRATE A PAGAN HOLIDAY

Christmas Redemption looks at some of the symbolism and traditions of Christmas, including gifts, the Christmas tree, and even Santa Claus and shows how all of these can be celebrated and enjoyed by Christians as a true and accurate reflection of the gospel.

Though Christmas used to be a pagan holiday, it has been redeemed by Jesus.

If you have been told that Christmas is a pagan holiday and is based on the Roman festival of Saturnalia, or if you have been told that putting up a Christmas tree is idolatrous, or if you have been told that Santa Claus is Satanic and teaches children to be greedy, then you must read this book! In it, you will learn that all of these Christmas traditions have been redeemed by Jesus and are good and healthy ways of celebrating the truth of the gospel and the grace of Jesus Christ.

REVIEWS

Too many times we as Christians want to condemn nearly everything around us and in so doing become much like the Pharisees and religious leaders that Jesus encountered. I recommend this book to everyone who has concerns of how and why we celebrate Christmas. I recommend it to those who do not have any qualms in celebrating but may not know the history of Christmas. I recommend this book to everyone, no matter who or where you are, no matter your background or beliefs, no matter whether you are young or old. –David H.

Very informative book dealing with the roots of our modern Christmas traditions. The Biblical teaching on redemption is excellent! Highly recommended. –Tamara

This is a wonderful book full of hope and joy. The book explains where Christmas traditions originated and how they have been changed and been adapted over the years. The hope that the grace that is hidden in the celebrations will turn more hearts to the Lord's call is very evident. Jeremy Myers has given us a lovely gift this Christmas. His insights will lift our hearts and remain with us a long time. –Janet Cardoza

I love how the author uses multiple sources to back up his opinions. He doesn't just use bible verses, he goes back into the history of the topics (pagan rituals, Santa, etc.) as well. Great book! –Jenna G.

JOIN JEREMY MYERS AND LEARN MORE

Take Bible and theology courses by joining Jeremy at
RedeemingGod.com/join/

Receive updates about free books, discounted books,
and new books by joining Jeremy at
RedeemingGod.com/read-books/